Walk!

Mallorca

(North & Mountains)

with

Charles Davis

DISCOVERY WALKING GUIDES LTD

Walk! Mallorca (North & Mountains)

Second Edition published January 2006
First published June 2004

Copyright © 2006

Published by
Discovery Walking Guides Ltd
10 Tennyson Close, Northampton NN5 7HJ,
England

Maps
Maps sections are taken from **Mallorca (North & Mountains) Tour & Trail Map** (Super-Durable Edition, ISBN 1-899554-93-9) published by **Discovery Walking Guides Ltd**

Photographs
Photographs in this book were taken by the author, Charles Davis, and Jeanette Tallegas.

Front Cover Photographs

Cala Deià (Walk 7)   **Coll Baix (Walk 43)**

Overlooking Es Molí   Puig de Maria (Walk 33)
from the Archduke's
Path (Walk 6)

ISBN 1-904946-19-4

Walk! Mallorca
(North & Mountains)
CONTENTS

Charles Davis was born in London, and has lived and worked in the United States, Sudan, Turkey, Ivory Coast, Spain and France. With the onset of middle age, he realised that the urge to roam was better satisfied by walking than bouncing about on the back of a lorry in the middle of the desert, and now divides his time between mountain tops, desk-tops and laptops. He is the author of numerous highly praised and wholly unpublished novels.

Jeanette Tallegas has spent thirty odd years labouring for the French education system, from which she has finally, gleefully, taken early retirement. Asked what she intends doing now, she resolutely replies, "Nothing". Nonetheless, she does follow the author up various gruelling mountains, frequently alarming younger walkers who seem to assume that remote and inaccessible places are the preserve of youth.

Charles Davis is also the author of:-

34 Alpujarras Walks	ISBN 1-899554-83-1
Walk! Mallorca (North & Mountains) (2nd Edition)	ISBN 1-904946-19-4
Walk! Mallorca West	ISBN 1-899554-98-X
Walk! La Gomera	ISBN 1-899554-90-4
Walk! La Palma	ISBN 1-904946-06-2
Walk! Andorraa	ISBN 1-904946-04-6
Walk! Axarquía	ISBN 1-904946-08-9
Walk! The Lake District South	ISBN 1-904946-16-X
Walk! Dorset	ISBN 1-904946-20-8

- published by **Discovery Walking Guides Ltd.**

INTRODUCTION

If you're at your wits end, or think you are, which amounts to the same thing, if you're dazed and confused by the noise of civilisation and the haste to get someplace where you find you have nothing to do, if busyness has swamped your brain with facts and science blinded you with gimmickry, then follow me to an island where calm reigns, where the men never hurry and the women never age, and even the sun and the moon move at a more leisurely pace: thus, paraphrased for the new millennium, begins '*La Illa de la Calma*', the famous celebration of Mallorca by the modernist painter and writer Santiago Rusiñol. Perhaps the men move a little faster nowadays and doubtless the women age like everyone else, but the need for respite is more acute than ever and Rusiñol's evocation of tranquillity is as true today as it was eighty years ago. Forget the clichés about cluttered resorts catering to mass tourism; forget package holidays where it's the client rather than the services that are packaged; forget the crowded concrete tower blocks and beaches crammed with baking bodies; Mallorca has reinvented itself and, in so doing, has recovered its original face, the stillness and beauty of which have enchanted generations of artists and writers, and have now turned the island into Europe's most popular warm island walking destination.

THE ISLAND

As with so much that is praiseworthy in Spain, we have Africa to thank for the Balearics, which are in effect the exposed tip of the Baetic Cordillera, squeezed out of the earth's crust during the middle Tertiary period when pressure from the African plate occasioned all manner of happy havoc along southern Europe's tectonic frontiers. Subsequent folding, faulting, and karstic erosion have moulded this raw material into a tormented landscape of sheer cliffs and deep holes, weirdly fluted rocks, razor sharp ridges and fissured limestone pavement. What nature provided man has perfected, dappling the austere rockscape with groves of olive, almond and orange trees, taming precipitous slopes with neat terracing, canalising springs and streams, building remote mountain farms and beguiling sanctuaries, and gathering in picturesque fishing hamlets and atmospheric villages, all of which are linked by a complex network of paths pioneered by farm-labourers, muleteers, pilgrims, charcoal-burners, lime-firers, and snow-gatherers. The last three are particularly important for us, as these were the rural industries that penetrated the more inaccessible corners of the island, leaving their brand not only in paths but in the form of *sitjes*, circular moss-covered charcoal hearths, partially interred *hornos de calç* or lime kilns, and *casas de nieve* (*casa neu* in Catalan) or snow-pits. A less constructive but more lucrative business that also left its mark was piracy, which lead to the construction of the coastal watchtowers that provide a focal point for several classic Mallorcan walks.

The variety of walks that has resulted from all this fervid historical activity is remarkable, ranging from gentle strolls down peaceful country lanes, through bucolic rambles on cobbled donkey trails and pretty canal paths, to pathless scrambles traversing dense woods, rough scree, deep gullies, and remote windswept plateaux. Walking in Mallorca, we wind through pine forested slopes above azure blue waters, enter narrow gorges with towering walls that nearly touch high above our heads, peer over gratifyingly frightful precipices, marvel at dizzying sea views, discover idyllic creeks where swimming seems not so much desirable as compulsory, encounter rock formations so artfully sculpted you'd swear they were carved by hand, and admire olive trees so old and gnarled they look like stage-props from a computer-generated fantasy film... In short, if you can't find a walk to suit your tastes in Mallorca, you may as well hang up your boots and take to gardening!

The best known walking area is the **Serra Tramuntana** stretching from **Valldemossa** to **Pollença**, and it is this range that is at the heart of our book. Although the routes described here are all 'low' mountain walks (**Puig Major**, the island's highest peak, is less than 1500 metres), don't underestimate them. These are serious mountains, the ground is rugged, and one runs all the usual risks of mountain escapades – nobody's going to be complaining the terrain is too tame.

AIM AND SCOPE

The book is aimed at a wide range of walkers, from holidaymakers who want to break the beach-bar-restaurant routine with a leisurely stroll, to dedicated ramblers determined to reach the most remote peaks. For technical reasons, largely to do with mapping and not having something the size of a table cloth wrapping itself round your head in a strong wind, we have limited ourselves to the northern half of the island, but this involves no great sacrifice, as the majority of Mallorca's best walking is to be had in this region. Apart from walks in and around the **Tramuntana**, we also feature some remarkable itineraries in the eastern peninsulas of **Alcúdia** and **Formentor**.

WHEN TO GO

Given the fierce heat of summer, September to May is the ramblers' season. Autumn and Spring are best for birdwatching, April and May for lovers of wild flowers. Winters are generally mild and dry, though snow is not impossible. If you're relying on public transport, schedule your trip for May or September.

GETTING THERE, GETTING ABOUT, GETTING A BED

Charter, charter, charter: only for a very long stay will it be worth bringing your own car rather than renting, since the ferry from Barcelona is costly - and with 80,000 hire cars available on the island, you should be able to find something to suit your budget.

Theoretically, buses are good, but in practice seasonal timetables (not designed for walkers) dictate hiring a car. The most useful bus for us would be the **Sóller-Lluc-Pollença** route along the C-710, but this only runs daily from May (officially, though sometimes it starts in April) to September, and on Sundays throughout the year. **Sóller-Deià-Valldemossa**, **Alcúdia** and **Pollença** are reasonably well served, and there's a good service between **Caimari** and **Lluc**. For up-to-date information, see the relevant websites in Appendix B. Given the terrain, the network of trains is limited, but there is a popular link between **Palma** and **Sóller**, and some of the southern approaches to the **Tramuntana** are also accessible by train.

One common way of doing the longer linear routes, is to return by boat. Given that most of our routes are loops, this is not obligatory, but many of our walks could be combined with boat trips to make one or two day walking tours. Relevant boats for one-day trips would be: **Port de Sóller – Deià**; **Port de Sóller – Cala Tuent/Sa Calobra**; **Port de Pollença – Formentor**; **Port de Pollença – Cala San Vicenç**; **Playa Alcúdia – Cala San Vicenç**; **Playa Alcúdia – Formentor**. A two or three day walking trip sleeping over in the **Lluc Monastery** and/or the **Tossals Verds Refuge**, could be combined with the **Port Pollença - Port Sóller** boat. Timetables available in all Tourist Information Offices. Also enquire in your hotel. Some hotels have their own boat taxi service.

Accommodation is plentiful and easily organised privately, on-line, over the phone or on the spot. The well-heeled walker (and I'm not taking about your boots!) should head for **Es Molí**, **S'Olivaret** or the **Hermitage**. Those with shallower pockets, could try one of the ordinary hotels and apartments listed in the appendices. Those with no pockets to speak of at all, can use the monasteries and refuges. There are no official campsites on Mallorca, though there are designated camping areas at **Lluc** and the **Pixarells** *Área Recreativa*, and camping is tolerated in most *área recreativas*. There's also a patch of land beside the road near **Orient** (km 8 PM-210) on which someone has taken the trouble to write '*Camping Publico*'.

THE WALKS

Traditionally many of the classic walking routes in Mallorca are one-way itineraries returning to base by bus or boat, but we have opted for loops on the premise that it's more relaxing to make your own pace and not be hampered by somebody else's timetable - some guidebooks advise readers relying on the bus to 'walk quickly'! Occasionally natural or man-made obstacles oblige us to return by the same route. Classic one-way itineraries are cited and cross-referenced between looped walks.

Timings are all 'pure', excluding snacking, snapping and simply standing still staring. It is highly unlikely you will complete any of these walks in exactly the time specified. Before you tackle the longer routes, time yourself against one of our shorter itineraries, then curse me for a slow-coach or a racing maniac as seems appropriate. Timings marked with a **U** are walks I did 'Unaccompanied', when I tend to walk a little faster. All global timings include the return unless otherwise specified.

If the length of some walks seems excessive, do not be dismayed. All itineraries are planned in such a way as to be easily broken up or curtailed. As a general rule, the first itinerary within each regional section is comparatively easy and a suitable test walk. The remaining walks are arranged according to a roughly geographical logic and not according to complexity, effort or difficulty. If you're new to mountain walking, don't be too ambitious to begin with. Pace yourself on some of the less strenuous walks and Short Versions before tackling anything too wild.

The paths are generally well-maintained and waymarked, usually with cairns rather than paint (though you frequently have to know a route exists and commit yourself before finding any waymarks). However, some of the less celebrated routes are neither maintained nor waymarked and some of the itineraries in this book don't follow any paths whatsoever! That said, there are no itineraries detailed here that don't at least have the odd cairn along the way.

However, since my routes do not necessarily correspond to the traditional walk, only follow waymarks when they are referred to in the text.

Beware of improvising routes along charcoal burners' trails unless you're prepared for off-path walking or are ready to turn back. Charcoal burners had other things on their minds than getting up to the good views and their tracks often come to an end at a *sitja* in the middle of nowhere. Cobbled donkey trails give the impression of easy walking, but be careful in wet weather, when the more popular routes polished by thousands of feet can be like ice rinks.

Despite pioneering popular holiday walking, Mallorca has been slow to catch up on the internationally recognised GR system of red-and-white waymarked paths. At the time of writing, the GR-212 or 'Way of the Dry Stones', a sort of pedestrian version of the C-710 between **Andratx** and **Pollença**, is being set up. The wayposts are in place, though no GR-specific waymarking has been done to date. For some mysterious reason, the wayposts have been painted red-and-yellow rather than the customary red-and-white. Presumably the same system will be used when the route is waymarked.

Variation in place names between different publications is terrible. If you're not using our map, beware. Given the complexity of much of the terrain and the impact of human activity, the descriptions are fairly detailed. I've tried to give enough detail for those who need confirmation they're on the right path, but not so much as to irritate more confidant pathfinders with superfluity. For ease of reference, street names at the start of walks are in bold text. *Italics* are used for *discrete Spanish words*, if also in purple, you'll find them explained in the glossary. Consistency rather than deficient vocabulary accounts for all climbs being 'gentle', 'steady', or 'steep'.

EQUIPMENT

Given the roughness of the terrain, most of these walks require good walking footwear, though for some of the shorter strolls on country lanes, trainers would be adequate. As ever in hot climates, sun hat, long sleeves and trousers are advisable, and even if your skin doesn't burn easily, it's best always to have long trousers in your backpack for the thorny undergrowth that often invades paths. Plenty of water is essential, a picnic generally preferable, waterproofs and a warm top or windbreaker advisable according to conditions. Walking poles are helpful for those accustomed to them and GPS will make walking some of the more obscure routes considerably easier. You should also consider carrying some antihistamine. The Processionary Caterpillars occasionally seen in the pine forests may look cute as they nose-to-tail their way across the trail, but they are a pest. Not only do they kill the trees, they can provoke a strong allergic reaction in some people, generally just a rash, but in extreme cases a potentially dangerous swelling of the throat. If you're prone to allergies, take a supply of antihistamine with you – syrup for kids, tablets for adults. (See the section on Walking Equipment for a more detailed discussion.)

PROBLEMS

Violent crime is rare, but petty theft is endemic. <u>Never leave valuables in your car</u>. The most notorious spots are **Cap Formentor**, the **Lluc** monastery car-park and, above all, the parking areas around the **Cúber** reservoir.

Access to private land can be a problem. As a general rule, we've excluded all walks where access is restricted or potentially controversial, and have added notes in each walk's introduction if we believe there may be access problems at the time or preparing this edition. If, despite our best efforts, we have chosen a route subsequently closed off, please let us know.

FLORA & FAUNA

Carritx (a word you will see frequently in the descriptions) is the pampas-like diss grass found all over the island. The classic trick with *carritx* is to stand on it with one foot and trip over it with the other. Otherwise, the most common or distinctive flowers and shrubs are Asphodels, Euphorbia (also called spurge), Pistacia (also known as mastic or lentisc), Myrtle, Thyme, Rosemary, Foxglove, Hellebore, Windflowers, Blue Tobacco, and enough orchids to merit a book to themselves. In April the island is awash with brilliant flowering Mimosa, Jacaranda and Judas Trees, but on the whole, the most common trees in the mountains are Pine, Holm Oak, Strawberry Trees, Almond, Oleaster and Olive, the last frequently incredibly ancient and contorted.

Mallorca is a bird watcher's paradise. **The Bóquer Valley** and **S'Albufera** wetlands are world famous, as is the Black Vulture frequently seen in the **Tramuntana**. Other birds to look out for are the Bearded, Griffon and Egyptian Vultures, Booted Eagles, Osprey, Kites, Kestrels, and Falcons (notably the rare Eleanor's Falcon). There are a tremendous number of brightly coloured finches and tits, and more seasonal visitors than I can even begin to catalogue. Thrushes, Swallows, Martins and Partridge are common, and you may also see the wonderfully endearing Hoopoe, with his comical crest and dipping, gravity challenged flight.

As for mammals, reptiles and amphibians, you will occasionally see grandiloquent multilingual notices announcing 'Big Game Hunting'. Don't be deceived. The last big game they had on Mallorca was when the local football team beat Real Madrid and the biggest game most locals get on their plate is a portion of kid culled from the thousands of wild goats that roam the mountains. Wild boar and foxes have long since been wiped out, and the pine marten, genet and feral cats the island boasts might as well have been for all the average rambler sees of them – roadkill for the most part. We saw one weasel, several shrews, and heard loads of toads and frogs, of which the most emblematic is the Mallorcan Midwife Toad. Snakes are rare and not dangerous. Sightings of whales and dolphins are occasionally reported. More details available from the **Lluc Serra Tramuntana** Information Centre.

EATING & DRINKING

It would be entirely possible to spend an entire year on Mallorca without eating anything more alien than bacon and eggs, but assuming you fancy something more adventurous, the following notes might help get you started.

Sopa (soup) *mallorquin* is pretty much a vegetable stew and a good filling meal in itself, while *sopa de matances* and *sopa de pescado* are respectively the meat and fish equivalents. *Allioli* is garlic mayonnaise and *fonoi marí* is pickled sea fennel. *Pa amb oli* is dear to the Mallorca sense of self, but is not that exceptional, just the usual bread and oil found everywhere else in Spain:

'just', I say – it's very good, especially with charcuterie or a few slices of *Mahon*, a salty hard cheese. *Arroz Brut* is the local paella, *tumbat* is a variation on the classic Mediterranean combination of aubergine and tomatoes, and *greixonera* is a casserole. Beef (*ternera*) is a waste of time, but pork (*cerdo* or *porc*) and lamb (*cordero* or *anyell*) are excellent. *Butifarra* or *morcilla* is black-pudding and *sobrasada,* a local speciality, is a kind of *chorizo*-sausage pâté. Sweets and puddings are generally factory-made, but it doesn't matter greatly as the oranges *(naranja*s) are superb. *Zumo de Naranja*, sold everywhere, is fresh orange juice. Where Mallorcans really excel though is at the baker's: *ensaïmada* are light breakfast pastries, often copied elsewhere in Spain, but rarely done as well. *Coca* is the local crumbly-based, vegetable-topped version of pizza (the green topping is a mixture of shard, leek and lashings of parsley) and makes an excellent picnic snack, as do the vegetable pasties (*cocarrois*), and meat and fish pies (*empanada*).

Given the island's popularity with Germans, there is plenty of good foreign beer available. Of the local varieties, the well-known San Miguel is a bit soapy and not nearly as good as Estrella, brewed by the Barcelona based Damm, who also produce the more potent Voll-Damm. Mallorcan wine can be excellent, notably those from the Binissalem denomination, our favourites being the *Autentico* and *Vino Veritas* of Jose L. Ferrer. *Es Cós* from Valldemossa is good, too. *Hierbas* is the local digestive, a herb flavoured anisette.

TOURIST STUFF

There are dozens of general books about Mallorca, but if you don't care to carry a small library round with you, the following suggestions might help fill in a day off. Assuming you're based in the north of the island, a trip on the **Sóller - Port de Sóller** tram is almost obligatory. The old train between **Sóller** and **Palma** is equally celebrated and could be combined with a visit to the splendid cathedral, restored by Gaudi with such good taste even the architecturally illiterate contemplate it with reverence. Besides the boats mentioned in 'Getting About', there are numerous other boat trips, most starting from **Palma** or **Port de Pollença**. The island is riddled with caves (a feature of limestone landscapes) and speckled with monasteries and hermitages, many of which are worth visiting. For details on all of the above, ask for the relevant pamphlets in any Tourism Information Office, where you should also be able to pick up a seasonally published 'Where to go' brochure detailing festivals and exceptional cultural events. Since you're a walker, you probably pamper your feet and Mallorca is a good place to buy shoes, either from factory outlets round Inca selling smart classic shoes, or ordinary shoe-shops selling *mallorquins*, the distinctive canvas and leather summer shoe with car-tyre soles, and *albarcas* the superbly simple prototype sandal. The real highlight for the walker though is the Bestard factory at **Lloseta**, where the best Spanish walking boots are made - as good as you'll get in Britain and considerably cheaper.

LANGUAGE

English is spoken in most bars, restaurants and shops, but once you're out in the countryside, it's Spanish, Catalan or pantomime. Everywhere, a few words of Spanish will take you a long way, and a few Catalan phrases even further. Mallorcan Catalan is a less harsh version of the mainland variety, as is the linguistic politics of the islanders, who are not disgruntled if they have to speak Spanish.

ACKNOWLEDGEMENTS

Thanks to IBANAT (the official conservation organisation in the Balearics) for fielding a small army of forestry workers, both professional and voluntary, who not only keep the paths clear and the *áreas recreativas* clean, but are unfailingly courteous and helpful. Special thanks to the staff of the Serra Tramuntana Information Centre at **Lluc**: for expertise, dedication and approachability, they cannot be praised too highly. In particular, thanks to Rafael Mas who, despite spending most of his day behind a reception desk, is always friendly and informative. Special thanks also to Oliver St. John who suggested numerous itineraries, including some that didn't make it into the book because they scared the bejeezus out of me. And, as ever, thanks to Jeannette Tallegas for keeping me fed, watered and approximately clean while I battered away at my keyboard; to Ros and David Brawn for pioneering several of the routes featured here and for helping to solve a surreal succession of technical problems that climaxed in the definitive technical problem, getting the computer pinched; and to Bati for condescending to be lugged over endless stiles.

SYMBOLS RATING GUIDE

3 our rating for effort/exertion:-
1 very easy   **2** easy   **3** average
4 energetic   **5** strenuous

approximate **time** to complete a walk (compare your times against ours early in a walk) - does not include stopping time

8 km approximate walking **distance** in kilometres

200m approximate **ascents/descents** in metres
850m (N = negligible)

circular route

linear route

risk of **vertigo**

refreshments (may be at start or end of a route only)

Walk descriptions include:
- timing in minutes, shown as (40M)
- compass directions, shown as (NW)
- GPS waypoints, shown as (Wp.3)
- **U** at the start of a walk shows it was done unaccompanied, so generally walked at faster speed

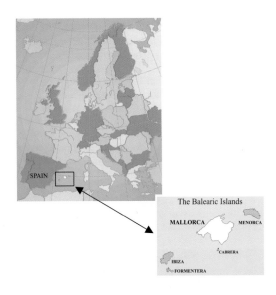

General area covered in the
Central Walks section
(Walks 9-27)

General area
covered in the
Western Walks
section (Walks
1-8)

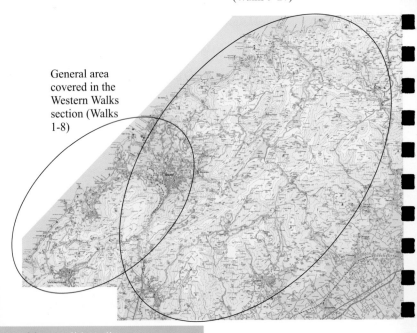

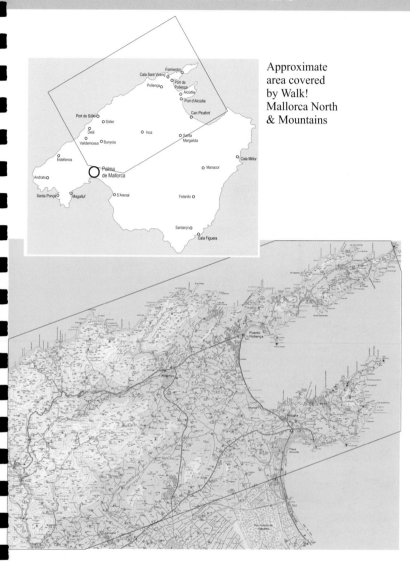

Approximate
area covered
by Walk!
Mallorca North
& Mountains

General area covered in the
Eastern Walks section
(Walks 28-44)

The map sections used in this book have been taken from **Mallorca (North & Mountains) Tour & Trail Super-Durable Map** (ISBN 1-899554-93-9) published by Discovery Walking Guides Ltd. All map sections are aligned so that north is at the top of the page. In the interests of clarity adjoining and inter-linking walking routes have been deleted from the map sections for each specific walking route. Waypoint positions, and numbers, refer to the walking route that the map section is illustrating.

Mallorca (North & Mountains) Tour & Trail Super-Durable Map is a 1:40,000 scale full colour map. For more information on DWG publications, write to DWG Ltd, 10 Tennyson Close, Northampton NN5 7HJ, England, or visit:

www.walking.demon.co.uk   www.dwgwalking.co.uk

ALTITUDE, HÖHE, ALTITUD, ALTITUDE

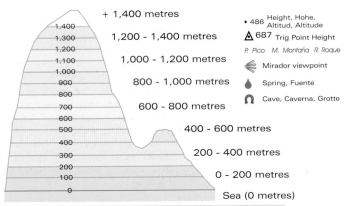

+ 1,400 metres

1,200 - 1,400 metres

1,000 - 1,200 metres

800 - 1,000 metres

600 - 800 metres

400 - 600 metres

200 - 400 metres

0 - 200 metres

Sea (0 metres)

• 486 Height, Hohe, Altitud, Altitude

▲ 687 Trig Point Height

P. Pico   M. Montaña   R. Roque

⬱ Mirador viewpoint

◖ Spring, Fuente

∩ Cave, Caverna, Grotte

ROADS, STRAßE, CARRETERA, ROUTE

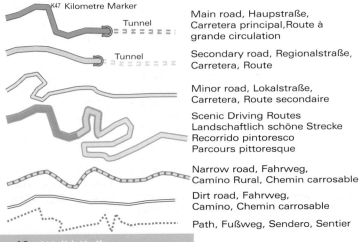

K47 Kilometre Marker

Tunnel

Main road, Haupstraße, Carretera principal, Route à grande circulation

Tunnel

Secondary road, Regionalstraße, Carretera, Route

Minor road, Lokalstraße, Carretera, Route secondaire

Scenic Driving Routes
Landschaftlich schöne Strecke
Recorrido pintoresco
Parcours pittoresque

Narrow road, Fahrweg, Camíno Rural, Chemin carrosable

Dirt road, Fahrweg, Camíno, Chemin carrosable

Path, Fußweg, Sendero, Sentier

Walking Routes, Wanderweg, Sendero, Chemin.

Walk Mallorca Route (Red)

🚶 17 ⑤ GPS Waypoint
see Waypoint Lists

🏰 Major Hotel 🏨 Important House, Casa Major 🏠 Hotel ⛽ Petrol

🏠 Forestry House, Casa Forestal 🏠 House, Casa 🏚 Ruin/Barn

🗼 Lighthouse, Leuchtturm, Faro, Phare 🍽 Bar/Rest

🗼 Tower, Turm, Torre, Tour 𝑖 Information Office P Parking, Parkplatz

⛪ Church, Kirche, Iglesia, Église ⛪ Chapel, Kapelle, Ermita, Chapelle

🪑 Picnic area, Rastplatz, Zona Recreativa, Pique-nique

[†] Cemetery, Friedhof, Cementario, Cimetière

[⚽] Sports Ground, Sportplatz, Campo deportivo, Terrain de sport

⛺ Camping, Campingplatz, Camping, Camping

🌬 Wind Turbine, Windkraftwerk, Eólica, Éolienne

USING GPS ON MALLORCA

The GPS Waypoint lists provided in this second edition of **Walk! Mallorca (North & Mountains)** guide book by Charles Davis, are as recorded by Charles during his research of the walk descriptions contained in this book. In the interests of clarity, each map section only shows the route and waypoints for that walk. Where a waypoint symbol is shown on a map it has been placed alongside the position to which it refers so as to not obscure the map detail and is numbered so that it can directly identified against the walk description and waypoint list. For readers wondering what we are talking about, GPS Waypoints are also Grid References to the exact locations within each walking route, when used in conjunction with the **Mallorca (North & Mountains) Tour & Trail Super-Durable Map**.

All The GPS Waypoints quoted in Walk! Mallorca (North & Mountains), and on the Tour & Trail Map, were recorded during the research of the walking routes, and are subject to the general considerations as to the accuracy of GPS units in the location concerned. Mallorca generally has good GPS reception with little 'mountain shadowing' causing reception problems. One exception is Walk 22, 'Three Pecks at the Torrent de Pareis' where GPS reception is non-existent within the gorge itself, so GPS waypoints are only provided for 22b above the gorge and on 22c for the descent into the gorge until GPS reception becomes unreliable. Walk 6 has poor reception on the descent to Deià, and Walk 16 'Tossals Verds Circuit' has two sections of poor GPS reception in the gorges encountered on the route. Walks 39 & 40 'Creek & Peak' routes have a section of poor reception as we ascend towards the main road. On these routes the lack of GPS reception are on sections of the walk where there is only one logical way and will not compromise your navigational accuracy. Occasionally Charles GPS track has had some discontinuities, caused we think by intermittent battery connection, but has produced a perfect track when the route has been re-walked. For our PNFs we are editing out the discontinuities and replacing them by the complete track.

It is virtually impossible to reproduce the exact GPS waypoint co-ordinates in practice when walking a route. While GPS waypoints are quoted to 00.0001 minutes of arc, in practice you should expect 10 metres as an acceptable standard of accuracy when you have '3D navigation' (four or more satellites in view); though good reception on Mallorca means that often your accuracy will be closer to 5 metres.

Signal Strength

Signal strength from sufficient satellites is crucial to obtaining an accurate location fix with your GPS unit. In open sky, ridge top, conditions you may have up to 11 satellites in view to give you a GPS location accuracy of 5 metres. Providing you have good batteries, and that you wait until your GPS has full 'satellite acquisition' before starting out, your GPS will perform wonderfully on Mallorca for all our routes, subject to the notes above on routes 16, 22 and 40.

To Input the Waypoints

GPS Waypoint co-ordinates are quoted for the WGS84 datum, used to provide grid references on the Tour & Trail Map, in degrees and minutes of Latitude and Longitude. To input the waypoints into your GPS we suggest that you:

- switch on your GPS and select 'simulator' mode
- check that your GPS is set to the WGS84 datum (its default datum) and the 'location format' 'hddd°.mm.mmm'
- input the GPS waypoints into a 'route' file with the same number as the walking route number; then when you call up the 'route' on Mallorca there will be no confusion as to which walking route it refers to.
- repeat the inputting of routes until you have covered all the routes you plan to walk, or until you have used up the memory capacity of your GPS; most GPS units will store up to 20 routes of up to 50 waypoints for each route, and you can always re-programme your GPS while on Mallorca.
- turn off your GPS. When you turn the GPS back on it should return to its normal navigation mode.

GPS Waypoints are provided as an additional navigation aid to complement the detailed walk descriptions in Walk! Mallorca (North & Mountains). Knowing exactly where you are in relation to our detailed walk description is a great confidence booster when exploring these new and exciting landscapes. GPS Waypoints are provided for all key navigational points on all walking routes; never again should you find yourself wondering whether you are on the right path or not.

Note that GPS Waypoints complement the detailed walking route descriptions in Walk! Mallorca (North & Mountains); and are not intended as an alternative to the detailed walking route description.

Personal Navigator Files (PNFs).

Edited versions of all the GPS tracks and waypoints compiled during Charles Davis' research are available as PNFs on our **Personal Navigator Files CD version 3.01**. GPS Utility Special edition software is included on the PNFs CD, enabling the user to load track and waypoint information direct to their GPS unit via a PC. In addition to **Mallorca (North & Mountains)** the PNFs CD version 3.01 contains the GPS tracks and waypoints for **Mallorca West**, **Menorca**, **La Gomera**, **La Palma**, **Tenerife**, **Lanzarote**, **Sierra de Aracena**, **Madeira**, **Alpujarras**, **Axarquia**, **Andorra**, and the full **Walk!**

UK series of guide books covering **Lake District North**, **Lake District South**, **Yorkshire Dales (North & Central)**, **South Pennines**, **Peak District South**, **Brecon Beacons**, **South Downs**, **Dorset**, **Dartmoor** and **Exmoor**.

The PNFs CD version 3.01 is available from Discovery Walking Guides Ltd at £9.99 including postage.

Confused by GPS?

If you are confused by talk of GPS, but are interested in how this modern navigational aid could enhance your walking enjoyment, then simply seek out a copy of **GPS The Easy Way**, the UK's best selling GPS manual. Written in an easy to read, lively, style and lavishly illustrated, GPS The Easy Way takes you through all aspects of GPS usage from absolute basics up to GPS Expert and debunking the myths about GPS along the way; an essential purchase for anyone thinking of buying a GPS.

"A compass points north" but
"A GPS tells you where you are, where you have been, and can show you where you want to go."
"Ask not 'What is GPS?' - ask 'What can GPS do for me?' "

GPS The Easy Way £4.99 is available from bookshops and post free from:
Discovery Walking Guides Ltd.
10 Tennyson Close
Northampton NN5 7HJ
www.walking.demon.co.uk & www.dwgwalking.co.uk

WALKING EQUIPMENT

Reading the postings on uk.rec.walking internet news group, it is obvious that walkers are very interested in the clothing and equipment used by other walkers. For some this interest borders on obsession, with heated debates over walking poles, boots versus sandals, GPS versus 'map and compass' navigation etc etc. Walking magazines are packed with clothing and equipment reviews, opinions and adverts, but few walking guide books give more than a cursory mention to recommended clothing and equipment. At the risk of upsetting some walking fundamentalists, here is a brief rundown on what I've used on Mallorca.

Backpack

A 25-30 litre day pack should easily cope with all the equipment you think you will need for a day's walking. A design with plenty of outside pockets to give easy access to frequently used items, such as ½ litre water bottles, is a good starting point. Well padded straps will spread the load and a waist strap will stop the pack moving about on the more adventurous routes. A ventilated back panel will help clear sweat on hot days and tough routes; a design with a stand-off frame is best for ventilation and worth the small increase in weight. Do spend time adjusting the straps so that you get the most comfortable fit.

As an alternative to traditional backpack designs, you might find the cyclist's packs produced by Nikko, and similar companies, a good compromise of stand-off frame, capacity, pockets and weight.

Footwear

Mallorca's dramatic landscapes offer no compromises, and nor should you compromise on your footwear. While there are many comfortable paths on the island, a lot of the walking is on hard rock, usually uneven. Whether you choose boots, shoes or sandals, they must be up to the task. You will need a hard sole with plenty of grip and a well padded foot-bed. My favourites are a pair of Bestard boots that I picked up at their factory shop on Mallorca. Worn with thick mountain socks, these boots have done everything I have asked of them. (Calzados Bestard, C/. Estación 40-42 Lloseta)

Whichever footwear you choose, do make sure that you have covered plenty of kilometres in them before coming to Mallorca.

Sun Protection

Always carry a comfortable sun hat, also useful should it rain. Choose a design that gives you plenty of shade, is comfortable to wear, and stays on your head in windy conditions. You will be spending several hours a day outdoors and sunburnt ears (and neck) are both painful and embarrassing. Sunglasses and high-factor sun cream are highly recommended.

Water & Food

Always carry as much water as you think you might drink. A couple of ½ litre bottles, a few pence each from local shops, is the minimum, and add another couple of litres for more demanding routes. Even on shorter routes, I would advise that you carry some survival rations. While some routes are well equipped with 'tipico' bars these may not be open when you need them, so survival rations of chocolate bars and the like can provide welcome comfort.

Medical Kit

Antiseptic wipes, antiseptic cream, plasters and bandage are supplemented by lip salve, which can seem like a life saver in hot dry conditions. Also include tweezers, which you will soon appreciate if you catch a splinter or cactus spine, and a whistle to attract attention if you get into difficulties.

Navigation

Do not compromise - buy the best guide book and the best map, and carry them with you. A compass is useful to orientate yourself at the start of a route and for general directions, but a GPS unit is far more useful - see Using GPS on Mallorca (P.17)

Clothing

Choose loose comfortable clothing and add a lightweight waterproof jacket to your back pack; the Balearic Islands are famous for sunshine but I saw quite a bit of rain while researching this book.

Other Equipment

You won't want to be carrying excess weight during your walking, especially on the longer routes with major ascents/descents. Digital cameras weigh far less than their film equivalents, and a monocular is half the weight of a pair of binoculars. Secateurs might seem an unusual choice of walking equipment, but they can be useful on some routes. A mobile phone, and money (refreshments, taxis, public telephones, drinks machines etc.) are also recommended.

PRAGMATISTS AND FANTASISTS

Ever since the thirteenth century and the birth of the mystic Ramon Llull, Mallorca has been a land of poets and dreamers, most of whom seem to turn up at the western end of the **Tramuntana**. But professors of otherworldliness rarely exist in isolation and the more romantic visitors to the island have always had to live alongside a profoundly pragmatic people. This combination of lofty ideals and matter-of-fact roots is manifest the minute you arrive in **Valldemossa** from the south.

Crossing the almond dotted plain on the PM-111, you get the strong impression you're heading for an impenetrable wall of mountain, but after the **Esporles** turning, a breach opens in the **Tramuntana**, and the road winds between olive and pine, climbing to the small valley around **Finca Son Brondo**, from where we get our first glimpse of **Valldemossa** and the western end of the **Teix** massif. A few moments later we see the monastery for which the village is famous. Perched on a pedestal of higgledy-piggledy terraces and surrounded by carefully tailored trees, it's the perfect emblem of Mallorca, a dream in stone, aimed at paradise but raised on decidedly earthy foundations.

Despite the village's development as a daytripper's haven, the impact of arrival probably hasn't changed that much since the Carthusians fell in love with Valldemossa in the fifteenth century and successfully petitioned King Don Martí (described by the Catalan writer and painter Santiago Rusiñol as "a man of such piety, nobody has a word to say about him, either good or bad"!) to give them the remains of the old royal palace.

Admittedly the monastery as it stands today is of relatively recent construction, but this must always have been a spot carefully balanced between heaven and earth, and the work the monks did over the next three centuries only serves to emphasize the dichotomy. When the order was disentailed in the 1830's, its properties throughout Spain were variously sacked by embittered tenants or sold into private hands. Being a practical people, the Mallorcans opted for the latter solution, renting rooms to rich tourists, for whom the simplicity of a monastic cell in the sun was a pleasing antidote to the dark satanic mills of the north.

The most celebrated of the monastery's guests were George Sand and Frederic Chopin, who visited Mallorca in 1838, hoping the island climate would improve Chopin's health. As it happened, an unusually dismal winter did more damage than good, a disappointment expressed in Sand's rather dyspeptic account of their season on the island, 'A Winter In Majorca'. To make matters worse, the Mallorcan peasant proved altogether too down-to-earth for the romantic nineteenth century imagination, resulting in some quite rancorous comments about the islanders. But the pragmatic nature that disappointed Sand has ensured her local immortality, and 'A Winter In Majorca' is now sold everywhere in every language.

Happier results came of the spot of bad weather encountered by the Archduke

Ludwig Salvador, a member of the Austrian royal family who preferred messing about in the Mediterranean to observing the more decorous rites of Viennese court life. Stuck in a rainstorm, the Archduke decided the only sane response was to buy a house, which he duly did, with the simple injunction that the owner, Señor Serra, name his price and make it fair as Ludwig wasn't a man to haggle and would only say yes or no. Being a pragmatic Mallorcan, Señor Serra named a fair price, so pleasing the Archduke he carried on buying farms for the next forty years, turning himself in the process into a one-man Mallorcan heritage industry.

Heading east from **Valldemossa**, we soon pass the first of the Archduke's purchases, **Miramar**. Loosely translated, miramar means 'Sea View', a name deceptively suggestive of a Sussex bungalow. As sea-views go though, **Miramar** is of a different order to anything found in England. Here the sea is so expansive and so invasive, reports from the 1930's suggest certain old men among the local population believed the island actually floated on the water, detached from any more solid mooring. And if testimony is required concerning the sea's colour, a deep, shifting camouflage of azure mottled indigo, one need only recall the story of a small boy who wouldn't go swimming because he feared turning blue.

After **Miramar**, the landscape opens out, the tightly packed pine and holm oak woods giving way to more spacious olive groves as we approach **Son Marroig** (another of the Archduke's country pads), beyond which **Puig Major**, the island's highest summit, and the rocky coast between **Deià** and **Sóller** come into view. Clustered round a small knoll tucked between the **Teix** massif and the sea, **Deià** has been located with considerable care, near enough to the exquisite little **Cala de Deià** for the purposes of communicating with the outside world, but far enough from the coast to have warning of marauding pirates.

In this instance, pragmatism played a hand that appealed to the romantics, too, and the village has attracted numerous artists and writers, notably the poet, novelist and mythologist, Robert Graves. Although the romance Graves espoused was of a different order to George Sand's, it was romance nonetheless, and it's no accident that a man who once went climbing with Mallory should end his days in **Deià**. There are several classic 'walks' here that I decided not include since they seemed closer to cliff face escapades than conventional rambling. **Deià** is now a popular tourist destination better known for its business magnates than its poets and can hardly be called the epitome of romance, but it's still visually stunning and remains sufficiently atmospheric to have one yearning for superficially less complicated times and the 'simple' life celebrated by more than one generation of romantic thinkers.

Leaving **Deià**, the narrow road curls along the contour line flanked by immaculately maintained terraces; and woe betide anyone in a hurry who happens to get stuck behind a bus and a pack of cyclists - overtaking is strictly for the suicidal and homicidal. Passing between **Can Prohom** and **Son Bleda**, we come to the western limit of our central section, the **Sóller** plain, home to the last, most local and most numerous of our fantasists.

Quiz show question: what's the world capital of oranges?
a. Seville   b. Valencia   c. Israel   d. Sóller

Most people would probably choose one of the first three options - unless they've already visited **Sóller**. The name comes from the Arabic for 'a golden shell', a suitably evocative description to give you an idea of this fertile valley, home to scores of small orange groves, the fruit of which has to be tasted rather than described. These oranges were the desideratum for the migrant dreamers of the **Sóller** diaspora, the adventurers that spread around the world in the nineteenth and twentieth centuries, working abroad for ten, twenty, forty years, however long it took to get the money to buy a patch of land at home and cultivate their garden. And all the while, they dreamed of the oranges they would grow, oranges so succulent and sweet, they remained bright in the mind's eye throughout forty years of wandering. It was a very Mallorcan dream, going away to get closer to home, seeing the world in order to settle on native soil - perhaps a pragmatist's fantasy!

WESTERN WALKS LOCATOR MAP

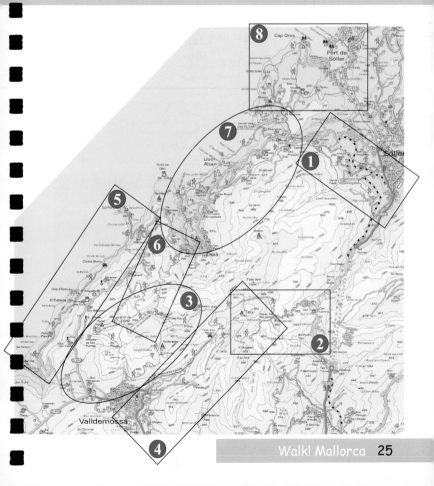

1 CAMÍ DE CASTELLO

This variation on the classic climb from **Sóller** to **Can Prohom** is an ideal introduction to walking in Mallorca. Following country lanes, cobbled donkey trails, dirt tracks and clear paths, it's easy walking all the way, winding between typically well-maintained terraces dotted with modest cabins and the occasional magisterial country home. Frequent shady passages mean this is a practical itinerary on a hot day, and a dense fringe of wild gladioli will reward flower-lovers in spring. If you're new to walking or don't fancy the steep climb at the start, the shortcut descents (see text) and stroll options are for you. More ambitious walkers can link to **Deià** and **Port de Sóller** (see Walks 7 & 8). The route is well-waypointed and the rights of way undisputed.

* + 20 minutes return to **Can Prohom**

Extension	Stroll
Turn left at Wp.7. Follow the dirt track for 50 metres then take the broad path skirting the field, arriving at the chapel just below **Can Prohom** (10M from Wp.7). See Walks 7 & 8 for longer excursions from this point.	Take the bus to **Can Prohom** for the descent back to **Sóller**
	Short Versions See text

Access: on foot from **Sóller**.

From the central *plaza* in **Sóller**, we take the **Avenguda de Jeroni Estades** towards the Tourist Office and turn first right on **Carrer de Isabel II**, which we follow until it ends at the roundabout at the southern tip of the **Sóller** by-pass (Wp.1 10M). 30 metres south of the roundabout, we cross the road and take the narrow concrete lane on the left of House No.6, **Vial 2 Pujol d'en Banya**. Climbing steadily, we bear left at **Can Domingo** and left again at the **Camí de ca ses Curiales** junction. Ignoring succeeding branches to left and right, we continue climbing on a slightly more moderate gradient. After levelling off for 200 metres, the lane winds through two S-bends before passing a cobbled trail on the left and swinging right (N) to cross the Palma-Sóller railway line (Wp.2 30M). From the level-crossing, the lane continues climbing steadily between terraces and the occasional cabin. After a final steep climb past House No.12, we leave the lane and bear right on a narrow path at a house with a large arched gate, signposted 'Camíno de Casteo (sic) por S'Heretat y Can Prohom' (Wp.3 45M).

After 100 metres level walking, the path runs into a dirt track. Ignoring two branches to the right (one minor, one major), we climb slightly to pass in front of a partially restored cabin and behind a carport, where the track dwindles to a path again. The path descends between terraces, passing several gates before dropping down steeply, then levelling out in the run up to a signpost for the first short return to **Sóller**, **Camí de Rocafort** (Wp.4 55M). We continue straight ahead on the **Camí de Castello**, which has recently been widened into a rough track here, damaging the wall defining the old path.

**Puig Major & L'Ofre
from below Can Prohom**

After a gentle descent, we climb behind a recently restored house, where we find a stretch of concrete and a waypost indicating we leave the track to recover the original narrow path (Wp.5 60M).

The path climbs steps crossing the **Cinc Ponts Torrent**, beyond which we cross a wayposted junction of dirt tracks. Maintaining direction (NW), we climb steeply on a rough concrete track, recovering the path 30 metres later at another waypost and painted rock sign in front of **Can Paies**. The path tunnels through a dense overgrowth of pistacia then continues through successive stretches of shade and sun, level and descent, before going through a rough wire gate. Strolling along immaculate terraces, we approach a large house fronted by a tall palm tree, just before which we come to our second shortcut option, a signposted path on the right, **Camí des Monts Reals** (Wp.6 70M).

To continue on the **Camí de Castello**, we go through the gated courtyard behind the large house, taking care to shut both gates behind us, after which a steady climb along a cobbled donkey trail brings us through another rough gate onto a dirt track between a small cabin and a stand of pine on a knoll topped with a gazebo. We bear right on the dirt track to maintain direction (NW), already in sight of **La Muleta** (see Walk 8). The track becomes a tarmac lane passing behind the luxurious **Cas Xorc Hotel**, at the gates of which (Wp.7 85M) we have a choice, turning left to continue along the **Camí de Castello** to **Can Prohom** and the longer extensions, or right to descend to **Sóller**.

Turning right for **Sóller**, we follow the wayposted dirt track, the **Camí des Rost**, past a first branch on the left (ending in a pleasant picnic spot if desired). The track then climbs towards a gate, just before which we bear left on a wayposted path (Wp.8 95M). After going through a rough gate, we join a cobbled path that soon broadens to a stepped donkey trail. Following a 100 metre stretch thinly coated with tarmac, we recover the cobbled trail which descends steeply to the junction with the **Camí des Monts Real** (see Wp.6). The cobbles eventually run into a tarmac lane, passing the junction for **Camí de Rocafort** (see Wp.4), 50 metres after which we bear left at House No.1 to rejoin the **Sóller** by-pass in front of the petrol station (115M). For the town centre, take the lane to the right of the petrol station.

2 TEIX from COLL DE SÓLLER

THE SAD DEMISE OF A ROUTE

Font de Teix and Sa Serra

I had just finished redrawing the map of our **Coll de Sóller - Teix** classic route when the news reached us that the access to this walk, always a bit iffy, had been completely sealed off. It seems this is an official policy of the bottling plant and land owners and it would appear unlikely that the Mallorcan authorities will intervene on behalf of a few walkers, even if those walkers make up much of the inland economy those same authorities are trying to sell to visitors.

Our former Walk 2 was introduced to us by Oliver and Eileen St. John and was first included in our Mallorca Mountains Walking Guide, then re-researched by Charles Davis for inclusion in Walk! Mallorca North & Mountains first edition. This is not the first route lost in this region. **S'Arrom** farm below the **Alfábia** ridge was the first to go. Then it was the Charcoal Burners' Trail, another St. John route below this one, originally in Mallorca Mountains Walking Guide but soon closed off after publication of our guide.

The loss of these routes is particularly sad as a great tract of unused landscape has been lost to walkers, Mallorca residents as well as visitors. Although various pressure groups exist on the island whose aim is to keep access open, they seem to have little success. It is easy to see a time ahead when lovers of Mallorcan walking will turn their back on these lost routes, giving up the battle with greedy landowners and uncaring authorities to exchange their allegiances for the walker-friendly destinations of the Canary Islands.

It goes without saying that walkers anywhere must exercise great care when exploring the countryside, respecting livestock, crops and property so as to avoid antagonising landowners, thus providing them with valid excuses to exclude walkers. And if walking in a group, it's the opinion of the publishers that the smaller the group, the better.

David & Ros Brawn

3 THE ARCHDUKE'S PATH from VALLDEMOSSA

In 1867 the Austrian Archduke Ludwig Salvator visited Mallorca and liked it so much he stayed, establishing a tradition that has continued unabated to the present day. Ludwig, however, was more ambitious than modern migrants. His season in the sun was conceived on a large scale and, rather than settling for a modest villa by the sea, he instigated a series of grandiose building projects, among them **Son Moragues** in **Valldemossa**, **Son Marroig** (see Walk 5b), and **S'Estaca** (see Walk 5a), the current retreat of Michael Douglas. Nor was Ludwig a man to take his rustic pleasures lightly. Instead of toiling along charcoal-burners' paths, he set about improving the **Teix** massif, laying a bridleway complete with refuges and *miradors*, a rich man's folly for which generations of walkers have been grateful. Parts of the path are a little too vertiginous for some tastes, but in this itinerary we visit the lower, less alarming stretch. Easy walking, ideal for a family excursion.

We describe two alternative loops: A: **Mirador de ses Puntes**, and B: via **Fontanelles**

A: MIRADOR DE SES PUNTES

| 3 | 2H* | 7 km | ⋀⋀ | 400m / 400m | ↻ | ⚠ | 0 | 🍴 |

* + 10 minutes if walking from the town centre to Wp.1

Extension	Stroll
Numerous possibilities, linking with Part B for a larger loop, Walk 4 to climb **Teix**, or Walk 6 to traverse the massif and descend to **Deià**.	100 metres after the stile, bear left over a line of stones to pass a dry spring and stroll along the wooded terrace above **Valldemossa**. Return the same way.

Short Version: To **Es Pouet**

Access: on foot from **Valldemossa** (accessible by bus from **Palma** & **Sóller**).

From the fountain car-park on the main drag through **Valldemossa**, we take **Carrer de la Venerable Sor Aina** towards the cemetery and football pitch, then second right onto **Carrer de Joan Fuster**, and first left onto **Carrer de les Oliveres**. If arriving by car, park at the end of this road.

The first ladder stile

From the **Oliveres** turning circle we take the gated dirt track (Wp.1 0M) for 150 metres until it is cut by a fence, where we turn left on a broad trail up to a wooden gate and ladder stile. Ignoring waymarked shortcuts immediately after the stile and after 20M, we follow the main trail as it climbs steadily through the wood to go through a wall gateway (Wp.2 30M) into the flat **Pla d'es Pouet**.

Carrying straight on through the woods for 200 metres brings us to the **Es**

Pouet well, where we bear right on a broad trail (NE). After a pleasant stroll through the peaceful woods we climb, gently then steadily, to the **Coll de s'Estret de son Gallard**, where we join the **Archduke's Path** (Wp.3 45M). Turning left, we soon come into fine views of the cliffs below the higher part of the bridleway. Continuing our climb, we see in succession the sea, the headland at **Port de Sóller**, and **Puig Major** and **Massanella**, before coming to the roofless refuge on **Puig Veia** (Wp.4 60M).

Following the cobbled bridleway, we pass the **Pover** trig point and a natural *mirador* overlooking the coast before descending to the decaying ramparts of the **Mirador de ses Puntes** (Wp.5 75M) where there are tremendous views across the **Valldemossa** plain towards **Galatzó** and, predictably enough, an equally tremendous drop. Five metres behind the *mirador*, the bridleway bears east for a gentle, shady stroll back to the well (90M), a little over thirty minutes from the start.

B: via FONTANELLES

We split the **Archduke's Path** into two because some people find the higher stretch a little vertiginous. To be honest, you'd have to suffer pretty acute vertigo to be disturbed by the drops here, which only inspired a mild toe-tingling in me: the cliffs are high, but the path is well made and flanked to the south by a gentle slope. As it happens though, pragmatic considerations have resulted in two walks we found more satisfying done separately than as a single itinerary. Better still, this gave us the opportunity to include the little known ascent via **Fontanelles**, a delightful climb that avoids queuing behind the large hiking parties ploughing up the traditional route. Apart from a few cognoscenti like Oliver St. John, who suggested this route, the only people you're likely to meet on this ascent are Mallorcans.

* + 40 minutes return for the short extension to Wp.5

Stroll	Extension
to the first *sitjes* b e t w e e n Wps.1&2.	Turn right at Wp.4 for the **Teix** (see text), right after Wp.6 for **Deià**, or carry straight on at Wp.8 for the **Mirador de ses Puntes**.

Access: on foot from **Valldemossa**

We start as for the **Mirador de ses Puntes**, but just before the stile, turn sharp right on a broad charcoal-burners' trail supported by a low retaining wall (Wp.1 5M), which climbs steadily, rapidly rewarding us with fine views of **Valldemossa**. After 15M the path levels out and goes through a wall gateway, from where it winds round a broad wooded valley. It then climbs again, becoming a little overgrown, before swinging left at a distinctive, triple-trunked pine for a final climb, varying from steep to steady, ending at a *sitja* and ruined shelter (Wp.2 45M).

Just behind the *sitja* in the trees to your right, you may notice a small cairn. If so, ignore it! This is one of the demented shortcuts impatient Mallorcans pioneer to confuse foreigners. Instead, we maintain direction (NW), leaving the *sitja* on our right. 10 metres later, cairns and old red waymarks indicate our way over the rocks onto an oak-wooded ridge. On our left 100 metres later,

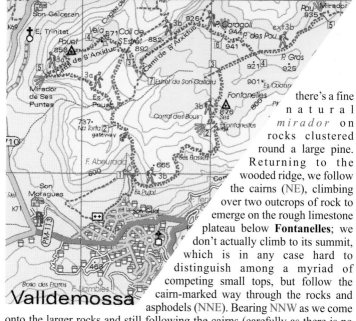

there's a fine natural *mirador* on rocks clustered round a large pine. Returning to the wooded ridge, we follow the cairns (NE), climbing over two outcrops of rock to emerge on the rough limestone plateau below **Fontanelles**; we don't actually climb to its summit, which is in any case hard to distinguish among a myriad of competing small tops, but follow the cairn-marked way through the rocks and asphodels (NNE). Bearing NNW as we come onto the larger rocks and still following the cairns (carefully as there is no other clear orientation point), we cross the plateau to join a branch of the **Archduke's Path** (Wp.3 60M) (NOTE: this path isn't normally classified as part of the Archduke's Bridleway, but that's what the locals call it and it was obviously laid at about the same time). Bearing right, we climb a gentle slope to join the main **Archduke's Path** (Wp.4 70M) next to a small stand of pine, at the heart of which is a small shelter built around the roots of a fallen tree.

Extension

For a short extension and/or to climb **Teix**, turn right and follow the 'motorway' (hopefully avoiding traffic jams) as it crosses a shallow depression before climbing to two small tops overlooking **Cala de Deià** and **Sa Foradada** (Wp.5 10M [from Wp.4] the second top). Continuing on the path for ten minutes as it zigzags down beyond the tops brings us to the junction with the path up to **Teix** (Wp.13 of Walk 4).

For the main walk

We turn left at Wp.4 and climb past a first small top to a knoll with a short access path, **Puig Caragoli** (Wp.6, 75M). A couple of minutes later, the **Archduke's Path** passes the cairn-marked descent to **Deià** (see Walk 6), after which we reach its 'vertiginous' stretch (a mere toe-tingler, I assure you) along the clifftops. The views are magnificent, most notably of **Sa Foradada** (see Walk 5). When the path starts zigzagging down through the pine trees, look for a branch to the right after about five minutes of descent, signposted with a small wooden panel suspended from the trees (Wp.7 110M), where we leave the main path and descend through the oak wood to the **Coll de s'Estret** and its V-shaped bench (Wp.8 120M [Wp.3 of alternative loop A]). To continue along the **Archduke's Path**, carry straight on (see above). Otherwise, bear left and follow the broad trail down through the wood to reach **Es Pouet** well in ten minutes. Bear left (S) to cross the *pla* and go through the wall gateway onto the red-waymarked trail back to our starting point in a little under thirty minutes.

Climbing the **Teix** from **Valldemossa** is perhaps *the* classic Mallorcan walk and can be a bit of a motorway with huge hiking parties strung along the horizon like a marching army. This variant, unpublished elsewhere, uses a slightly less well trod route. Well, to be honest, parts of it are almost completely untrod apart from mountain goats and a few eccentrics like ourselves, so you need excellent pathfinding skills or a GPS 'GoTo' function and a strong desire to get off the beaten track - well off it! Less venturesome souls should opt for the Easy Version.

N.B. The **Serra des Cairats** is called **Serra de Son Moragues** on some maps.

Short Version	**Extension**	**Stroll**
Follow the Easy Version (see text) to Wp.9 then turn right for some pleasant cliff-top picnic spots on the mossy *sitjes* between Wps.9&8	Turn right at Wp.13 to link up with the **Archduke's Path**, Walk 3.	Follow the main **Cairats Valley** track until it starts to climb.

Access: on foot from **Valldemossa**

We start from the playground on the PM-111 at the eastern end of **Valldemossa** (Wp.1 0M). 100 metres along the PM-111 (dir. **Palma**), the pavement ends at a bottle bank and we climb the stairs on the left.

Turning right to pass the house with a castellated tower, we follow **Carrer Lluis Vives** into **Carrer Xesc Forteza**. 100 metres past a bushy carob tree on an island in the road, we bear left on a dirt track signposted 'Refugi' (Wp.2 10M).

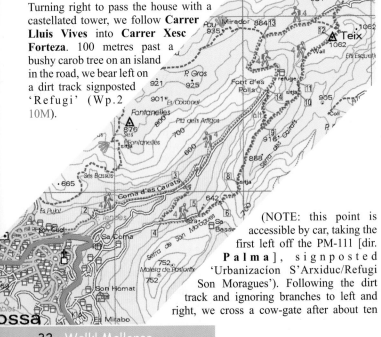

(NOTE: this point is accessible by car, taking the first left off the PM-111 [dir. **Palma**], signposted 'Urbanizacíon S'Arxiduc/Refugi Son Moragues'). Following the dirt track and ignoring branches to left and right, we cross a cow-gate after about ten minutes, where we bear left into the **Cairats Valley**. Two hundred metres later, shortly after a ruined *caseta*, we leave the main dirt track to take a branch track doubling back on the right (SW) (Wp.3 25M).

Easy Version

To avoid all pathfinding difficulties, stay on the main dirt track up the **Cairats Valley** to the **Font des Polls** picnic area in the **Son Moragues Área Recreativa**, where a 'Serra des Cairats' signpost (Wp.14) indicates a broad trail on the right up to Wp.9 (15-20 minutes from Wp.14). It's virtually impossible to get lost en route to the picnic area, except at the first S-bend two minutes after Wp.3. If you've missed the waymarked shortcut, ignore the track straight ahead at the first curve of the 'S'.

Full Version

Following the branch track as it winds up the hillside (SW), we turn left at a T-junction marked by a large cairn and pinkish waymark (Wp.4 35M). 50 metres later, we bear right on a broad trail below a retaining wall before stone steps bring us across a second wall to rejoin the dirt track. Continuing along the dirt track (E), we go through a gap in a wall, where the track forks into two narrow paths (Wp.5 45M). Taking the path on the right, we climb through another gap in the wall onto a narrow woodland path. Turning left, we follow new pink waymarks up through the wood (E). Ignoring a cairn-marked branch on the right leading to a cave, we climb onto a mini rock-fringed plateau, beyond which we find more pink waymarks before crossing the tip of an old wall. The path is fainter here, but we bear right 15 metres after the wall and, following the pink waymarks, cross a pathless stretch onto another, almost level, and much clearer woodland path (Wp.6 55M). Turning left, we wind through the woods for five minutes to a *sitja* where the path disappears and the difficult bit begins!

Crossing the *sitja*, we find two cairns. Bearing right just after these cairns, we come onto a faint 'way' (ESE) marked by the occasional cairn. Roughly 75 metres after the *sitja*, a small cairn propped against the base of a tree on our left, indicates the start of our pathless climb through the woods. Following the cairns, we climb very steeply on loose soil and acorn shells up to a sloping rock sheet, bringing a wall above us into view. We climb straight up and, about 50 metres below the wall, bear left to cross it at a freshly broken down section (Wp.7 80M). There's no path beyond the wall and no cairns, but a path is not far away. After climbing directly up from the wall for about 30 metres, we bear left (NE) to skirt the rocky outcrop of the ridge. We soon reach a *sitja* and the ruins of a shelter (Wp.8 90M), from where, 50 metres to the NE, we glimpse the tell-tale moss of another *sitja*, beyond which there is a good level path.

Following this path (NNE), we cross a couple of low retaining walls, after which another cairn-marked route climbs from the left (an alternative route from the *sitja* after Wp.6). Passing several *sitjes* and ruined shelters, we soon glimpse the **Teix** above the treetops, after which we descend slightly before running into a U-bend in the broad trail from the **Font des Polls** picnic area (Wp.9 100M).

Bearing right here (left on the Easy Version) we climb steadily till the trail ends at the last *sitja* (Wp.10 115M), where a rough stony way dotted with cairns and red waymarks climbs (E) to a wall topped with a fence. Bearing left, we follow the wall for 50 metres before crossing it by a second waymarked breach (Wp.11 130M). Frequent cairns and waymarks guide us up a steep, but easy climb across the rocks (not recommended in descent) (NE) to a gap in the wall girdling the southern side of the **Teix**, from where it's a gentler climb to the trig point on the summit (Wp.12 150M).

From the peak, we descend (ENE) to the *coll* between the **Teix** and its sister peak, where we bear left (NNW) down to the **Pla de sa Serp** plateau. Following the broad obvious trail (WNW) we cross a slight rise to a Y-junction just before a wall. The two branches rejoin beyond the wall for a final rocky descent to a large pile of stones on the **Archduke's Path** (Wp.13 165M). Bearing left, we follow the well-stabilised path zigzagging down to the **Son Moragues** refuge (locked, but there's a covered terrace behind it with a fireplace), where the broad dirt track begins. 200 metres later, we come to the **Font des Polls** picnic area and the Easy Version 'Serra des Cairats' branch (Wp.14 190M).

Valldemossa

The track now descends steeply, passing the open-air museum (partially restored *sitjes*, lime-kilns, and a bread oven). The gradient eases off and we leave the **Son Moragues Área Recreativa** via a stone-stepped stile. 200 metres later, a waymarked shortcut on the right brings us through the S-bend at the bottom of the climb, just short of Wp.3, twenty-five minutes from **Valldemossa**.

5 SA FORADADA

A: THE LOST PATH

Sa Foradada is the classic picture-postcard peninsula between **Deià and Valldemossa**. For many years this attractive coastal route was dubbed the **Camí Perdúa** or 'Lost Path' after half of it fell into the sea. If you do the whole thing you may conclude it's still lost as the exhausting rock-hopping route pioneered by local ramblers couldn't be called a 'path' even by the most panglossian hiker. But the first half is very easy, an ideal family excursion, and the second half is at once a geologist's dream and a happy regression to childhood for those who have fond memories of messing about on rocky beaches when they were kids.

*   Full version 4, Short Versions (a) 2 (b) 1
**   + 20 minutes for the extension
       Short Versions (a) 1¼ hours return, (b) 1½ hours return
*** At the **Sa Foradada** bar - if it's open

Short Version	**Stroll**
(a) to **Cala S'Estaca** (b) to Wp.5	To **S'Estaca** house and back
Version (a) is the more attractive option, but the steep descent (and re-ascent!) and deep waters at **S'Estaca** mean (b) is preferable for families, even though it's longer. If bathing at **Codols-Blancs**, 'jellies' or plastic sandals are advisable.	**Extension**
	To **Cala S'Estaca**. Groups with two cars could combine (a) & (b) to avoid doing the 'lost' bit both ways.

Access: by car. Take the PM113-1 to **Port de Valldemossa**. There's room for one large or two small cars just before and again just after km3.6. At a pinch, there's a parking space for one small car at the next sharp bend.

To start, we go down the road and turn right, just before km4, onto the **Sa Marina/Font Figuera** concrete track (Wp.1 0M). The track passes three houses and two gates, the second of which may be shut but can be passed by a pedestrian gate to the left (Wp.2 15M). Shortly after the second gate, we ignore a waymarked path descending to the left and continue on the concrete, soon coming into view of the white towers of the **S'Estaca** house, built by the Archduke Ludwig Salvator and now owned by the film star Michael Douglas. (N.B. This is not the extension!)

After climbing behind the well-tended vineyards of **S'Estaca** (it's a wonder the man has time to make any films) we start descending, ignoring a cairn-marked path climbing to the right, and getting our first sight of the **Sa Foradada** peninsula. When the concrete track bears sharp left between two pillars (Wp.3 30M), usually chained off, we take the dirt track branching right.

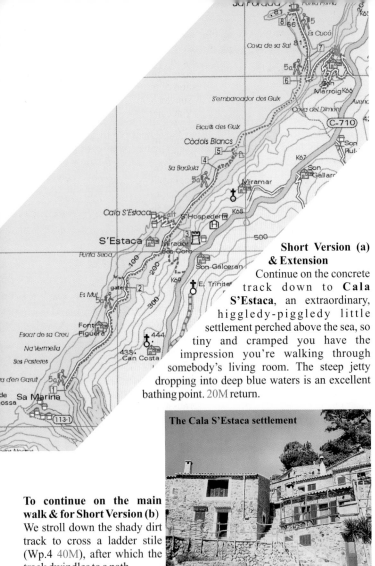

Short Version (a) & Extension

Continue on the concrete track down to **Cala S'Estaca**, an extraordinary, higgledy-piggledy little settlement perched above the sea, so tiny and cramped you have the impression you're walking through somebody's living room. The steep jetty dropping into deep blue waters is an excellent bathing point. 20M return.

The Cala S'Estaca settlement

To continue on the main walk & for Short Version (b)
We stroll down the shady dirt track to cross a ladder stile (Wp.4 40M), after which the track dwindles to a path.

The path descends to a *sitja*, where it doubles back to the left (NW) to a large rock with red-painted requests not to leave litter (Wp.5 50M). Just behind this rock is an idyllic picnic spot with benches and a table.

The onward route isn't very long but it is exhausting and every step of the way is a potential disaster: don't continue in trainers unless you've got elephant ankles. My two companions wisely chose to stay on the stony **Codols-Blancs** beach. But for those of you who are happy hopping from rock to rock…

To continue on the lost path
We bear right, as indicated by red arrows, to pass the ruins of a cabin. Ignoring the clear path branching right from the cabin, we bear left to descend steeply

past a fallen pine down to a cairn. We then pick our way across the rocks and descend onto the stony **Codols-Blancs** *cala*.

What follows is no harder than crossing the *cala*, but it is remorseless and you'll end up drenched with sweat. A couple more cairns lead us out of the *cala*, after which it's essentially a question of more of the same, scrambling over the larger rocks, hopping over the smaller, dabbing the sweat from your eyes and looking out for those ankles. You can't get lost as **Sa Foradada** is directly in front of you, but when the way isn't obvious, look for the cairns indicating the easiest route. And do stop once in a while. One can be so busy watching one's feet, it's easy to forget the huge 'eye' at the tip of **Sa Foradada** ('drilled' or 'pierced') which gradually comes into view. After a good, or possibly not so good, fifty minutes of hopping along the rocks, we recover the old path (Wp.6 100M), either passing under a fallen pine to climb directly onto the path (not obvious) or scrambling up a slope to a cairn 30 metres later. The path widens almost immediately to a trail that joins the main track down from **Son Marroig** (Wp.7 105M) where we bear left and stroll along to the neck of the peninsula (Wp.8 115M [see Wp.3 of the **Son Marroig** descent]). Returning by the same route takes about 1½ hours excluding the extension (don't ask why, but it <u>was</u> quicker uphill!).

B: FROM SON MARROIG

Son Marroig is another of the Archduke Ludwig's country pads and can be visited as part of this easy walk for those who don't fancy the gymnastics of The Lost Path. An ideal walk for a misty morning when nobody else is about and the mountains are under cloud. Some books say you need to ask permission to go down (confirmed by notices at the start) others that permission is implicit in purchasing a ticket to visit the house. We couldn't find anyone interested in giving us permission and the bar-keeper said we didn't need it.

Access: by car or bus (km 65.5 C-710)

From the main doors of **Son Marroig** (Wp.1 0M), we walk up the tarmac lane (SE) past the lion-head fountain and, 50 metres later, climb over the ladder-stile at the green 'No-pasa-sin autorizacion' gate. Following the initially concreted track on the other side of the gate, we bear right at the Y-junction a couple of hundred metres later.

The stony track winds down past superb cliffs that look like they're melting, passing yet another *mirador* constructed by the Archduke, a man for whom a good view was never enough, before it is joined by the track leading to The Lost Path (Wp.2 35M). After strolling along to the neck of the peninsula (Wp.3 45M), we have a choice between a swim from the **Playola** jetty, a drink in the bar (rarely open before midday), or (not recommended since only climbers can descend to the hole) a scramble onto the **Foradada** rock itself. We return by the same route (85M).

This complicated ascent from the **Hotel es Molí** is not well known and rarely appears on maps, let alone in guidebooks, which is baffling because it's a superb route, while the descent along the **Caragoli Camí des Cingles** is, metre for metre, probably the most spectacular <u>path</u> on the entire island. I can only suppose the pathfinding difficulties on the way up and the apparent impossibility from afar of the descent have discouraged previous researchers. Fortunately, locals have been more tenacious and the charcoal burners' paths we use on this itinerary have been kept opened and marked (to a greater or lesser degree) with cairns. This is another suggestion for which we have to thank Oliver St. John. The descent should not be undertaken when visibility is poor and I recommend gaining some familiarity with the **Archduke's Path** on one of the easier ascents from **Valldemossa** before tackling this itinerary.

N.B. There may be hunters at weekends in the hunting season in the next estate; you might see their hides from above **Son Rullan** around waypoint 8.

Stroll	Extension
- to Wp.4	See Walks 3 & 4 for **Teix** and/or traverses to **Valldemossa**

Access: on foot from **Hotel Es Molí** at the western limit of **Deià**. Ask permission to use the hotel car-park.

Overlooking Hotel Es Moli

From the top of the hotel car-park (Wp.1 0M), we climb the tarmac lane behind the hotel, passing above the swimming pool and winding through two hairpin bends, after which the tarmac gives way to a dirt track. Ignoring a concrete branch on the left, we continue along the dirt track towards a farmhouse, 50 metres before which we bear left on a cobbled path marked with cairns (Wp.2 10M) and gateposts that resemble wayposts from a distance.

The cobbles give way to a dirt path leading, after 50 metres, to a rough barrier of two wooden palettes. Clambering over the palettes, we recover the cobbled path and climb past occasional blue and red arrows. The path, which switches between cobbles and dirt and is sometimes overgrown with *carritx*, was part of the network giving access to the abandoned terraces behind **Hotel Es Molí** and can be confusing due to branches onto individual terraces. There are at least two cairn-marked routes across the terraces, so don't worry if you see cairns off your path. Just follow the right bank (our left) of the small valley (SW), looking for cairns every 50-75 metres.

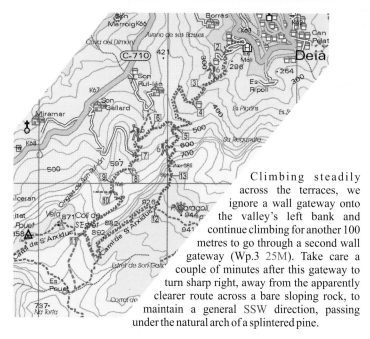

Climbing steadily across the terraces, we ignore a wall gateway onto the valley's left bank and continue climbing for another 100 metres to go through a second wall gateway (Wp.3 25M). Take care a couple of minutes after this gateway to turn sharp right, away from the apparently clearer route across a bare sloping rock, to maintain a general SSW direction, passing under the natural arch of a splintered pine.

At a small cabin (Wp.4 40M) fronted by a small trough carved into the rock, we bear right onto the northern side of the valley, either passing below or above (the two paths rejoin) a dry tunnelled spring

Fifty metres after the two paths rejoin, we bear left on another cobbled section leading to a cascade of terraces. After 30 metres, the cobbled path rejoins a dirt and stone path, and we bear left to go through a long, lazy, shallow zigzag. Bearing left again, away from rusty metal gates, we follow a level track, which soon climbs gently into the oak forest.

Ignoring a major branch to the left, we continue climbing and, 75 metres later, bear sharp right, passing a small red waymark to climb steadily to a first *sitja*. Bearing right again, we climb past another, larger carved trough (there were some <u>very</u> patient people living up here), 30 metres after which the main path swings left.

We leave the main path here, bearing right onto a second *sitja*, just beyond which there's a small bread oven (Wp.5 60M). This is an important junction. Sensible, linear-minded people will turn sharp left immediately after the bread oven and follow the cairn-marked route up to **Puig Caragoli**. The rest of you can follow me!

Crossing a line of stones and branches intended to prevent precisely this sort of thing happening, we maintain direction (W) on a clear, level path that soon dips down and bears left (SW) to a gap in a fence/wall flanked with a lime-kiln and an octagonal carved stone basin (Wp.6 65M). Ignoring the track through the gap in the wall, we bear left, staying on the near side of the fence/wall, bringing the superb **Son Rullan** farmhouse into view. Fifty metres later, we go through a gate in a lateral fence and descend two large natural rock steps. Passing another carved trough, we continue alongside the main fence/wall for

100 metres to a large *sitja* at the end of a dirt track, which, 50 metres later, joins a larger stony track climbing from **Son Rullan**.

Bearing left, we follow this track up through two hairpin bends until it levels off at the remains of another large *sitja*. Cairns on our left indicate a way up through the trees, but it's easier to continue on the track, passing a small bread oven, 40 metres after which, as the track bears right, we turn left onto a charcoal burners' trail (Wp.7 75M). The trail climbs steadily, passing *sitjes* and the very occasional cairn, before virtually disappearing at a final *sitja* and ruined shelter (Wp.8 85M).

Cairns just above the *sitja* lead us onto a faint trail that climbs to cross and recross an old wall 50 metres later. We then climb alongside the wall for less than 50 metres to a small flat area, where the faint trail we've been following completely disappears. Twenty five metres further on, cairns indicate 'ways' to right and left. Ignoring the way to the right toward a *sitja* (it ends above heartrending cliffs), we bear left following three large cairns onto some very rough, very faint terraces (ESE). After crossing the first two 'terraces', we bear right to find a very faint trail through the woods to a wall (Wp.9 95M). Crossing the wall and bearing slightly left, we climb a tiny rise to come into sight of the wooded **Coll de s'Estret**. A faint path now descends (SSE) to another *sitja*-shelter-oven combination. Five metres behind the bread oven is the clear stony trail (Wp.10 100M) that leads up to **Col de s'Estret**. The pathfinding difficulties are over!

We turn left (away from the *coll*) and start climbing. The trail soon swings back towards the *coll* and climbs steadily in a southerly direction. Finally we clamber over a broken wall and, 50 metres later, come to the v-shaped bench at the *coll* (Wp.11 125M). Turning left, we follow the **Archduke's Path** onto the top of the cliffs, where it dips and rises along its most spectacular section.

After a long steady climb the path levels off in full view of **Puig Major** then bears right (ESE) towards the distinctive rocky knoll of **Puig Caragoli**. Just before the path dips down into the shallow depression before **Caragoli**, we find a large, metre high cairn on our left (Wp.12 155M) indicating the start of our descent. NOTE: if clouds have formed across the valley above **Deià** (which can happen alarmingly quickly) either return by the same route or take one of the easy descents to **Valldemossa** and catch a bus back. This is no place to be blundering about in the mist looking for a path.

To our left, a clear stony trail descends to another large cairn, where it seems to drop off the edge of the cliff – don't worry, it doesn't: this isn't a sick joke. Leaving the **Archduke's Path**, we follow the clear stony trail (NNE) down towards the first oaks, where the path again appears to drop off the edge of a cliff – this time it does, almost! Bearing left after a long outcrop of rock next to a black/white private hunting sign (Wp.13 165M [there are no more waypoints due to poor GPS reception]), we follow the meticulously cairn-marked route down to a broad wooded traverse descending steeply below a first stretch of cliff. This and subsequent descents are all easy and rarely vertiginous, but take care as the rocks are unstable underfoot.

At first, the path has been built up in zigzags, but we soon descend directly along the face of the cliff (this sounds alarming, but the trees and 20 metre broad traverse mean it's a relatively easy descent) before bearing left to emerge from the first belt of trees onto a broad open stretch overlooking **Son Rullan** and **Sa Foradada**. Another built up stretch of path bears right, bringing us into a stand of mixed pine and oak, where we begin another long sloping traverse below cliffs and between trees. At the end of the second line of cliffs, the path narrows and doubles back to the left again, passing a large rock with a cairn on top and a man-made step with an old gatepost built into the rock.

We now come into the main oak forest, where we follow a long northward traverse, climbing slightly before continuing our descent. Ignoring a branch on the left, we turn sharp right, still following the cairns, to pass the final cliff face. We then zigzag steeply down through the woods to the bread-oven *sitja* at Wp.5 (205M) where we rejoin our outward route, forty minutes from the start. It's worth pausing on the way down in front of the rusty metal gates to look up and contemplate what is, from here, an evidently unfeasible descent.

If you're doing this path for the first time in descent as part of a traverse from **Valldemossa** (not recommended) bear right and cross the bread-oven *sitja* to descend the broad trail beyond it. Ignore a main branch doubling back on the right and continue along the cairn-marked way down to the olive terraces. After doubling back from the rusty gates and descending through the long, lazy zigzag, look out for the cobbled path descending on the right. Bear sharp left at the small cabin to descend alongside the valley.

A classic route winding along undulating coastline (take your swimming costume) and returning on one of the most popular paths in Mallorca. The path toward the end of the coastal walk is complicated, but well marked with red dots and cairns.

Short Version	Stroll	Extension
Cala de Deià to **Es Gall**, returning via the same route	**Camís de Sa Vinyetta** and **Ribassos** Loop	See Walks 1 & 8 for links to **Sóller** and **Port de Sóller**

Access: on foot from **Deià**

From the eastern end of **Deià**, just beyond the main car-park, we take the tarmac lane on the left, signposted 'GR Sóller/Cala de Deià Camí de Sa Vinyetta' (Wp.1 0M). At the end of the lane, we cross a stile onto a cobbled trail descending through olive terraces, crossing the road to the *cala* three times before joining it just above the **Camí des Ribassos** wooden bridge. Ignoring the GR-212 for **Sóller** on the right, we stay on the road down to the *cala*. At the chain blocking car access to the beach (Wp.2 30M), we can either bear right or descend to the beach, just above which long stone steps lead to an intersection where the path from Wp.2 runs onto a terrace. Bearing right behind a stone cabin on the eastern spur of the *cala*, we follow a low clifftop, climbing onto the next terrace when the path disappears.

At the first *mirador* (below a 'Cuidado con el perro' sign), we cross a watershed where a steel cable and ladder help us over a fallen tree (Wp.3 45M). Passing a picnic spot with a stone bench and round table, we climb to follow a high retaining wall, before crossing a wooden stile into a pine forest. A second stile brings us into woodland devastated by processionary caterpillars and *tomico*, a wood-boring bug that can kill a tree in 15 days flat! After a breach in a stone wall (Wp.4 70M), we descend to pass in front of a house next to the sea. The path then levels out, passing between another house and small *mirador*.

After the next stile (Wp.5 80M), we bear left to squeeze between the branches of a fallen tree and climb stone steps toward a steep earth cliff. The path across the cliff face has disappeared, obliging us to climb till we're level with the second of several deep terraces, where a newer path bears left. Another eroded stretch (passable at the time of writing, but not for long), means we have to zigzag up to cross the watershed causing the erosion, immediately after which we bear left to recover the main path. Passing between two cairns, we ignore a waymarked route climbing to the right and continue along the coastal path, crossing a dramatically riven gully. Once across the gully, we follow a fainter path marked with cairns every 10-15 metres.

After a winding climb round a logjam of dead trees, we again ignore waymarks to the right, and bear left below a huge boulder to climb onto a

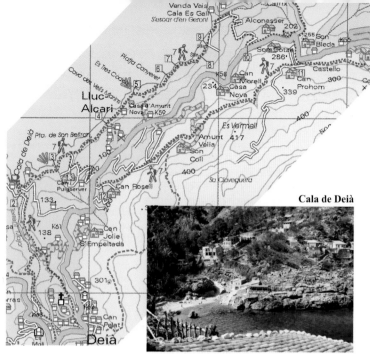

Cala de Deià

small wooded ridge. We then descend steeply alongside a wire fence, which we cross via a stile (Wp.6 95M) to rejoin the path cut by the logjam.

Crossing terraces of gnarled olive trees, we ignore old waymarks to the right yet again (Wp.7 100M) and follow newer waymarks and cairns down towards the sea. A sinuous path then climbs through a partially cleared tangle of dead trees to emerge at a stile (Wp.8 110M) behind orange and grey cliffs backed by a deep fissure. The path becomes clearer and broader, traversing well-tended olive terraces to a padlocked gate and a stile (Wp.9 115M) leading onto a dirt track. We descend along the dirt track for 75 metres before bearing right on stone steps climbing into the woods, on the far side of which we join the concrete lane between the **Alconasser** estate and **Cala Es Gall** (called **Venda Vais** by locals). Turning right, we climb steadily along the lane for twenty minutes before joining the C-710 (Wp.10 145M).

Turning left and staying on the left-hand side to face the traffic, we follow the road for 500 metres, passing the **Bens d'Avall Restaurant** turning (link to Walk 8), after which we cross the road to take the dirt track in front of **Cas Sord**. After 15 metres, we bear left, climbing to **Can Carabasseta** and a tumbledown chapel, where we join the GR-212 (link to Walk 1) and turn right on a cobbled path up to **Can Prohom** farmhouse (Wp.11 165M).

After crossing the front yard of **Can Prohom**, we bear left on a dirt track for 150 metres before bearing left again on a wayposted path. The path goes through a green gate and crosses dense woodland before passing above two houses. After crossing an access track, we descend along a cobbled trail then climb newly paved steps to pass in front of **Son Coll** (**Posada del Rey Jaume**). Descending along dirt paths and ignoring a branch path to the left, we follow a broad low wall to emerge behind a new house (**Can Rosell**).

Bearing right on a roughly surfaced lane, we descend to join a smoother tarmac lane where indications for **Deià** and the GR have been scratched onto a concrete wall (Wp.12 210M). We can either follow the GR to the left on a cobbled path or bear right on the tarmac lane. Both emerge 50 metres later on the C-710, where all waymarking miraculously disappears!

The GR turns left, following the C-710 for 700 metres before descending to the **Camís des Sa Vinyetta** and **Ribassos** junction. **Deià** is 1.6km along the road. To minimise road-walking we turn right, and then 100 metres later, left into the **Son Beltran** *urbanización*. Ignoring the 'Prohibido El Paso' sign, we follow the *urbanización* road down to a Y-junction. Bearing right toward **Can Oliveras**, we come to another 'Camíno Particular/Prohibido El Paso' sign, on the left of which steps lead down to a path below a wall with blue paint on the corner (Wp.13 225M). We follow this path to rejoin our outward route 150 metres east of Wp.3, ten minutes from **Cala de Deià**.

To return to **Deià**, we take the wooden bridge (ten minutes from the *cala*) onto the **Camí des Ribassos**. The cobbled trail soon becomes a dirt path climbing across terraces to join a paved way between houses and a lemon grove. The access track for the houses leads to a tarmac lane which we follow to the second Y-junction. Turning left past House No. 3, then left again in front of the **Deià Archaeological Museum**, we follow **Calle Felipe Bauza** up to the main road, 200 metres from our starting point, twenty-five minutes from the wooden bridge.

La Muleta plateau is popular walking country, but recent *urbanizaciónes* bring the risk of routes becoming blocked to walkers, and some landowners can be less than welcoming; even so, some of the routes detailed below should remain open. Given the optional routes, timings from Wp.8 start at 0M.

* or 1½h (via Wp.3-7) +1h return if starting from **Port de Sóller**
** from **Port de Sóller** returning via **Rocamar Hotel**, 3h (2¼h via Wp.3-7)

Short Versions	Strolls
(i) via **Rocamar Hotel** to Wp.11, return via Wp.15 **(ii)** drive to Wp.10 via the C-710, do one of the loops from the top	**(a)** from Wp.1, bear left then first left again up to the **Muleta** plateau **(b)** drive towards **El Faro** and, after the **Hotel Brisas**, take either of the access roads on the left through the aborted **Muleta** *urbanización* (the second is better surfaced). Park in the first turning circle (Wp.15) at the end of a *cul-de-sac*. A broad, cairn-marked path joins the red waymarked route just below Wp.12 (5M). Turn left to explore the plateau.
Extension see Walks 1 & 7 to **Sóller** & **Deià**	

Access: by car or on foot from **Port de Sóller**. Park below the restaurant, not in the restaurant car park.

Crossing the stile at the western end of the **El Faro** restaurant car-park (Wp.1 0M), we ignore a minor path on the left and follow the main path down towards the coast. After crossing a pine-forested rise, the path passes a branch on our right marked by a large cairn, 10 metres after which, at a major crossroads on a large sheet of rock (Wp.2 15M), we have a choice of routes, one spectacular and (almost) pathless, the other, on well-trodden paths..

Spectacular and Pathless (50 minutes)
Continuing straight ahead, we cross a small valley. Climbing a narrow, cairn-marked path, we go through a breach in a wall next to a large uprooted pine, where the path briefly disappears.

The rock shelter at Punta Sóller, 35 minutes into the route.

Bearing right, we follow cairns across an outcrop of rock to recover the path as it winds between more rocks. After scrambling up a rocky slope we see on our right the **Panxeta** overhang, resembling a melting rhinoceros, after which we reach the clifftops at **Punta Sóller** where there's a nicely hollowed rock shelter and, to the left, a large cairn marking the descent into the next valley (Wp.3 35M).

Picking our way down the rocks behind the cairn, we come to a natural terrace from where more cairns indicate a way across the valley to two boulders bracketing a path climbing on the other side (Wp.4 45M).This path is narrow

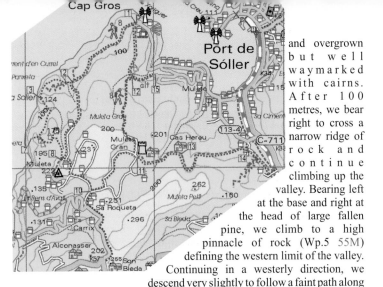

and overgrown but well waymarked with cairns. After 100 metres, we bear right to cross a narrow ridge of rock and continue climbing up the valley. Bearing left at the base and right at the head of large fallen pine, we climb to a high pinnacle of rock (Wp.5 55M) defining the western limit of the valley. Continuing in a westerly direction, we descend very slightly to follow a faint path along an abandoned terrace. The path descends onto the next terrace, from where we see an 'eye' in the sharp rocks ahead of us. A flurry of cairns (Wp.6 65M) lead up to a long nose-like rock tipped with a 'horn', 40 metres behind which there's a roofless stone cabin. Bearing right behind the 'nose', we scramble over rocks (not the sharp ones with the eye, but the rounder rocks on the left with a pine growing between them) into a rocky basin backed by a low sloping natural 'wall' (Wp.7 75M) with excellent views of the coast towards **Deià**. To continue, we return to the roofless cabin.

After going through a cairned breach in the wall to the left of the cabin, we bear right on an old path to a second cabin 40 metres away. Bearing left (SE) on a virtually pathless route marked with cairns, we come to a third ruin with a large pile of stones in front of it. The cairns disappear, but maintaining direction (SE), we pass 15 metres to the right of a fourth partially restored cabin fronted by a pile of breeze blocks and descend between rocks into a badly overgrown valley. Following animal tracks through the *carritx* (E), we cross the valley and bear right (SE) to climb across abandoned terraces, then continue climbing across better maintained terraces (SSE) up to a rough track, recognisable from below by the tooth-like stones set in the retaining wall (Wp.8 100M), where we bear right.

Quick & Easy (15 minutes, from Wp.2)

Turning left, we climb across two limestone outcrops. After a crumbling wall we bear right, crossing a terraced swale before bearing right again at a large wall running north-south. Following cairns, we cross a succession of shallow terraces until we see to our right (Wps.3-7EZ) a small cabin and a distinctive well, faced with a rudimentary wire gate. The traditional route continues climbing here and is still marked with cairns, but is in the process of being privatised. Bearing right, <u>away</u> from the cairn-marked route, we take the path <u>in front of the well</u>, passing two restored cabins before joining the rough dirt track leading to Wp.8. From Wp.8 0M, the track climbs past a small house to join another better stabilised track (Wp.9 5MN.B. There's a fence crossing the track at Wp.9 with a 'Private - No Entry' sign, serving only to inhibit those heading <u>to</u> the lighthouse, but not <u>from</u> it. The fence is movable to allow the passage of traffic, with a loop over the pole at one end.)

We bear right then left on a third, broader track. When the third, main track swings right, we take a branch track to the left (Wp.10 10M) ignoring an old 'Camíno Privado, Prohibido el Paso' sign (**for Can Prohom** stay on the main track and bear left at the next junction to join the C-710 at the **Bens d'Avall** turning, see Walk 7). 150 metres later, our branch track comes to a Y-junction. DO NOT TURN RIGHT unless you like being shouted at! Turn left, to go to the north of the **Muleta de Cats Avinyons**, the house with the distinctive squared tower, where we come to a crossroads of dirt tracks (Wp.11 20M) and another choice of routes.

To return to El Faro

We turn left towards the gated field and cross the wall by metal spike steps. Following the main track through the field, we bear left 50 metres from the gate then right 100 metres later, soon after which the track dwindles to a narrow path winding through the *carritx*. This complicated path is easy to follow as it's almost over-marked with cairns, red dots and blue arrows. At a large cairn/line of stones (Wp.12 45M), we ignore the wider branch to the right and bear left following the red dots. 20 metres later a major branch to the right leads to the lower of the two turning circles at the top of the **Muleta** *urbanización* (Wp.15), an alternative return to the port. Continuing on the red route, we cross the terraced gully of the **Raco de s'Argentera** and climb slightly to pass behind a roofless ruin, heading for the electricity cables (NNE) connecting the **Muleta Refuge**, the roof of which is soon visible. To the left of the refuge, we join the minor path 40 metres from our starting point, fifteen minutes from Wp.12.

To descend to Port de Sóller from Wp.11

We continue straight ahead on the main track, bearing right after 20 metres to follow a narrower track that circles the house before dwindling to a path. Behind the house, we bear sharp left and go through a gate into an olive grove. Descending through the olive grove, we join a partially cobbled donkey trail down to the **Muleta de ca s'Hereu** farmhouse, offering orange juice and *pa amb oli* (Wp.13 10M from Wp.11).

Following the signposted route ('Sóller' but in fact **Port de Sóller**), we continue along the cobbled trail. After a stone bridge over a watercourse, we go through a metal frame gate to descend through a second olive grove (E), which we leave by another metal gate with a notice requesting we shut the 'door' (sic). We then follow the cobbled trail down to the derelict **Rocamar Hotel**. Bearing sharp left at a junction just above a spindly carob tree (Wp.14 30M), we take the dirt track crossing the hotel premises to join the PMV-113-4. 300 metres on the left is the **Campo Sol Restaurant**; 200 metres beyond that, the sea front.

If you're doing this route in reverse

To reach the **Rocamar Hotel** from **Port de Sóller**, walk along the sea front (W) and turn left just before the **Bar Las Delicias II**.

If you're returning to Sóller,

The path continuing south from Wp.13 joins the C-711 at km 33.7 (Wp.16 35M).

See the notes on GPS use and waypoints on pages 19-20.

1.

Camí de Castello

Wp	N	E
1	39 45.6721	2 42.6912
2	39 45.2974	2 42.3102
3	39 45.5458	2 42.3068
4	39 45.7617	2 42.0042
5	39 45.7690	2 41.6959
6	39 46.0175	2 41.5215
7	39 46.3014	2 41.1119
8	39 46.2871	2 41.5943

2.

Teix from Coll de Sóller

Wp	N	E
1	39 43.9368	2 41.1438
2	39 43.7910	2 40.3182
3	39 44.0268	2 40.2678
4	39 44.0448	2 39.7590
5	39 43.8780	2 39.6810
6	39 43.7118	2 39.7266
7	39 43.5990	2 39.6126
8	39 43.4838	2 39.5364
9	39 43.4370	2 39.6588
10	39 43.5252	2 39.8628

3.

The Archduke's Path from Valldemossa

(a)

Mirador de ses Puntes

Wp	N	E
1	39 42.8682	2 37.3145
2	39 43.2654	2 37.2762
3	39 43.7040	2 37.3362
4	39 43.7490	2 37.1406
5	39 43.5360	2 36.7278

(b)

via Fontanelles

Wp	N	E
1	39 42.9702	2 37.3788
2	39 43.2852	2 38.0232
3	39 43.5642	2 38.0910
4	39 43.6992	2 38.3196
5	39 43.9146	2 38.8392
6	39 43.7970	2 38.1108
7	39 43.5792	2 37.4784
8	39 43.7040	2 37.3362

4.

Teix from Valldemossa

Wp	N	E
1	39 42.6834	2 37.3776
2	39 42.8334	2 37.7964
3	39 43.0554	2 38.5590
4	39 42.8250	2 38.3442
5	39 42.8730	2 38.5986
6	39 42.9156	2 38.7978
7	39 43.0254	2 38.9676
8	39 43.0518	2 38.9652
9	39 43.3782	2 39.1416
10	39 43.5348	2 39.4020
11	39 43.6110	2 39.3804
12	39 43.8792	2 39.6816
13	39 43.8810	2 39.1368
14	39 43.5534	2 39.1482

5.

Sa Foradada

(a)

The Lost Path

Wp	N	E
1	39 43.2106	2 35.6020
2	39 43.7832	2 36.0546
3	39 44.1432	2 36.4296
4	39 44.4612	2 36.7638
5	39 44.5482	2 36.8760
6	39 44.9682	2 37.4220
7	39 45.1134	2 37.4958
8	39 45.3528	2 37.3404

(b)

from Son Marroig

Wp	N	E
1	39 45.0768	2 37.7574
2	39 45.1194	2 37.4928
3	39 45.3540	2 37.3422

6.

The Archduke's Path from Deià

Wp	N	E
1	39 44.7900	2 38.6304
2	39 44.6958	2 38.4282
3	39 44.5326	2 38.2584
4	39 44.4204	2 38.1438
5	39 44.3136	2 38.0610
6	39 44.3166	2 37.9014
7	39 44.1588	2 37.7268
8	39 44.0850	2 37.6884
9	39 44.0250	2 37.5702
10	39 43.9518	2 37.5618
11	39 43.7202	2 37.3488
12	39 43.8696	2 37.9332
13	39 44.0370	2 37.0334

7.

Deià - Can Prohom - Deià

Wp	N	E
1	39 44.9388	2 38.9058
2	39 45.5502	2 38.4960
3	39 45.7050	2 38.7294
4	39 45.9594	2 39.1398
5	39 46.1322	2 39.3438
6	39 46.2300	2 39.5946
7	39 46.2924	2 39.6750
8	39 46.3428	2 39.8466
9	39 46.4016	2 39.8982
10	39 46.3944	2 40.1814
11	39 46.2900	2 40.5966
12	39 45.5874	2 39.0684
13	39 45.7236	2 38.8428

8.

La Muleta

Wp	N	E
1	39 47.8170	2 40.8546
2	39 47.5110	2 40.3776
3	39 47.4096	2 40.1088
4	39 47.3568	2 40.1538
5	39 47.3004	2 40.1742
6	39 47.2488	2 40.1490
7	39 47.1762	2 40.0608
8	39 47.0856	2 40.3140
9	39 47.0334	2 40.3722
10	39 46.8768	2 40.5006
11	39 47.0988	2 40.8414
12	39 47.5140	2 40.8090
13	39 47.0892	2 41.1756
14	39 47.1072	2 41.7654
16	39 46.9716	2 41.9724
3-7EZ	39 47.2794	2 40.4160
15	39 47.5374	2 40.9974

FROM THE GOLDEN SHELL TO THE SEA OF ROCK

Though friendly and helpful, I suspect the people of **Sóller** mistrust outsiders. I suggest this only because the town's one-way system is like something out of an M.C. Escher drawing. Things look straightforward enough when you arrive, but venture into town by car and you'll find yourself going in completely the wrong direction to get where you want to go. Either the locals are out to protect their privacy or they've decided the town's narrow streets can only cope with local traffic and have elaborated a road system so complex it baffles all but the most stubborn tourist. - all to the good, as this is a place to explore on foot. Apart from the museum, Botanical Gardens and a few distinguished buildings, there's not much in the way of classic sightseeing, but it's a delightful little town of sunny, bustling streets and shady peaceful alleyways, with several good bars and restaurants, and a central plaza, ideal for whiling away an afternoon watching the world go by - and when you tire of the human parade, a short stroll to the edge of town unfolds the fabulous spectacle of the surrounding mountains.

If you approach **Sóller** from the south, you'll be confronted by a toll tunnel, a boon for local people, reducing what was, with repetition, a tiresome, time-consuming climb to a straightforward, fast road. However, if you're not in a hurry, take the old road snaking over the **Coll de Sóller**. The bends are interminable, but so, from certain strategic points, are the attractive views, even on a cloudy day. And if you don't have a car, the nonagenarian train from **Palma** is an essential excursion.

Virtually anywhere else in Spain, the plain between **Sóller** and the port would be a dense forest of tower blocks or a broad sweep of villas. There's some development, but the passion for oranges, orchards and gardens has saved this area, and there are several attractive strolls to be done. **Port de Sóller** is very much a tourist resort with the usual array of bars and restaurants and car-hire outlets, but on an eminently manageable scale, at once peaceable and affordable, used as much by locals as visitors.

The C710 heading east from **Sóller** is one of the island's great drives/cycle rides. Snaking its way up past the celebrated **Mirador de ses Barques**, it climbs towards the daunting summit of **Puig Major**, an increasingly dramatic gulf opening out between the road and the long ridge sealing the **Cúber** and **Ofre** valleys. After the **Sa Bassa** *área recreativa* a sea of rock unfurls around us, announcing the approach of the first of two tunnels boring through the fringes of **Puig Major**. Beyond the tunnel, we are in the heart of the sea, with the white crest of **Puig Major** towering over a long trough backed by bubbling waves of rock. With their usual pragmatism, the Mallorcans have taken advantage of the terrain to turn this spot into the region's principal water storage point; once again, practical considerations have had an aesthetically pleasing outcome. Girdled by small mountains, **Cúber** reservoir is a picture postcard lake, a metallic mirror changing colour from steely green to deep aquamarine according to the humours of the sky. After **Cúber** we begin the long eastern descent, passing **Gorg Blau** reservoir (lower down but the source of most of the water in the **Cúber**) and going through the second tunnel, where the wave breaks, and a cascade of rock tumbles down toward **Pollença**. First though, there's an essential detour to the left, the extraordinary descent to **Sa Calobra** and **Cala Tuent**, which in a couple of kilometres, passes through a narrow defile just above **Nus de Corbata** - The Tie Knot. One glance at the map tells you all you need to know about the subsequent descent. No matter how many mountain tracks or corniche routes you've done, you won'e fail to be impressed by this road, frequently so tightly coiled it resembles a partially unravelled spring. And if you can take your eye off the road for a fleeting second, you'll see an equally impressive spectacle on either side, a gallery of remarkably varied rock, some delicately fluted, some mimicking the phantasmagoric shapes of Dali's Cap Creus, one striking declivity pinching the road like a peg, all of it quite stunning, especially in the twilight. The road is not for nervous drivers, though, boasting more bends than a plateful of spaghetti, narrow and used by unfeasibly large coaches. Professional drivers seem perfectly relaxed as they swing their buses (not to mention a ceiling full of screaming sightseers) r o u n d disturbingly

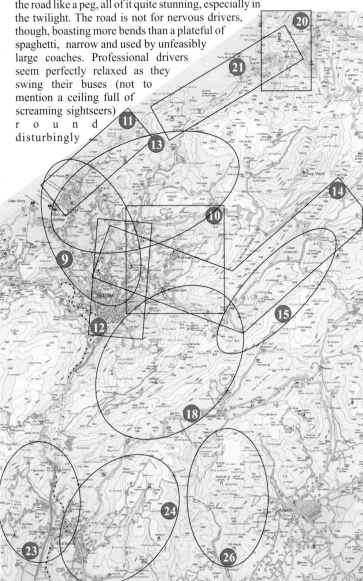

tight corners, but given that you're the one who must give way, often in places where there doesn't appear to be any 'way' into which to 'give', visiting motorists may wish to go early or late - above all, avoid this road at midday when countless coaches carry their cargo down to the feeding places at **Sa Calobra**.

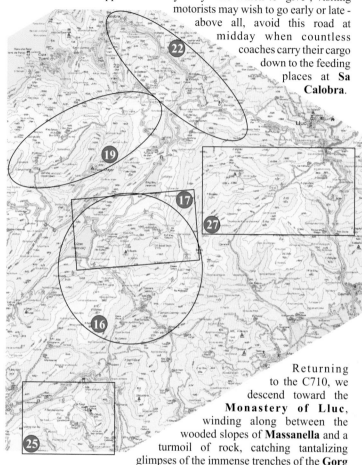

Returning to the C710, we descend toward the **Monastery of Lluc**, winding along between the wooded slopes of **Massanella** and a turmoil of rock, catching tantalizing glimpses of the immense trenches of the **Gorg Blau** and **Lluc** torrents, backed by the massif of **Puig Roig**, identifiable by the isolated **Quartel de Carabiners** barracks. The two torrents merge below the **Escorca** restaurant to form the single, indisputable natural wonder of the island, the **Torrente de Pareis**, a deep, narrow gorge debouching at **Sa Calobra** (inspiring the convoy of coaches mentioned earlier) and luring canyoning aficionados from all over Europe.

Parallel to all this drama, on the southern side of the **Tramuntana** between **Bunyola** and **Caimari** is an altogether gentler but no less beguiling landscape of pleasant, fertile valleys fringed with attractive woods and punctuated by impressive limestone escarpments. Long neglected by conventional tourists, its popularity is increasing making it quite crowded at weekends, but there are some great walks here and the tiny, winding lanes linking the villages are a gift to cyclists and motorists who are in no hurry to arrive.

Taking the **Alfábia Ridge** (Walk 18) to be a 10 on the testosterone scale, this delightful country stroll on tranquil lanes and quiet dirt tracks, must be about minus 6. Ideal for holidaymakers who aren't walkers, but fancy a walk to break the beach-bar-restaurant routine.

1 | 3H | 12 km | 370m* / 370m | 3

*very gentle inclines

Short Version	**Extensions**
Either route one-way, returning via the tram.	From **Port de Sóller**, link-up with Walk 10 returning from the **Mirador de ses Barques** via Walk 13. From **Sóller**, link-up with Walk 8 and return via **Can Prohom** (see Walk 1) or join Walk 11.

Access: on foot from **Port de Sóller** or **Sóller**

Starting at the eastern end of **Port de Sóller** next to the **Altamar** snack bar (Wp.1 0M), we follow **Carrer Antoni Montis** past the **Hostal Es Port** where it runs into the PMV-2124.

After a gentle climb of a little over a kilometre, we wind round the **Es Figueral** hamlet and continue our steady ascent through an increasingly rural landscape, gradually coming into view of the **Coll d'en Marques** and, beyond it, the round topped cliffs of **Es Cornadors**. A final climb between terraces of olive and carob (the bean of which is such a regular size and density, it's the source of the carat valuation of gold) brings us onto **Coll d'en Marques** (Wp.2 40M) from where we glimpse **Sóller** church.

After a gentle descent past the local recycling plant and more terraces, we emerge on the C-710 (Wp.3 60M). Bearing right, we descend 250 not very pleasant metres to the **Sa Teulera Restaurant**, where we turn left and take the initially unnamed lane (**Camí de ses Argiles**) beyond the recycling bins towards **Sóller**. At the junction with **Camí de Can Domatiga** (a possible shortcut if you don't want to go into **Sóller**), we bear left on a narrow, busy lane that eventually joins our return route at an inverted Y-junction (Wp.4 80M).

Sóller's main *plaza*

To continue into Sóller
Bear left, passing the **Bar Buenos Aires**, the football ground and **Fornalutx** road (Walk 10). At the end of the **Avenguda d'Asturies**, continue onto **Carrer de la Victoria 11 Maig**, then turn right at the T-junction with **Carrer de sa Lluna** to reach the central plaza (90M). To return to **Port de Sóller**, retrace your steps to Wp.4 (100M).

If starting in Sóller

Take **Carrer de sa Lluna** next to the BBVA bank in **Plaza de sa Constitució**, then second left, **Carrer de la Victoria 11 Maig**. Go straight on at the crossroads and bear right at the bridge (signposted 'Piscina Municipal') into **Avenguda d'Asturies**. Ignoring the **Fornalutx** road, carry on past the football ground and **Bar Buenos Aires** to the Y-junction, signposted on the right 'Lluc, Calobra, Port, Deià' (10M).

At **Wp.4**, we take the left hand branch of the Y-junction, a one-way street barred to outgoing traffic. At the next, staggered crossroads (**Camí de Can Domatiga** for the shortcutters), we continue straight on, heading for the square spire of a church. When the road bears left in front of the church, we maintain direction on **Camí de sa Figuera** to the C-710, which we cross with care - cars whip round the next bend at hell of a lick. We continue along a narrow tarmac lane signposted 'Finca Can Penya'. After 150 metres, we bear right at a Y-junction onto the **Camí de Son Lampaies** (an alternative spelling to the more common 'Lampalles'). The lane climbs gently between houses, cabins and orchards, bringing us to a Y-junction with **Camí de Can Baixo**, where we bear left for a slightly steadier climb on concrete, past the hens, guinea-fowl and turkeys of **Can Penya**. 100 metres later, at the **Can Penya** car-park, the tarmac gives way to a dirt track.

Ignoring a gravelled branch to the right, we climb through the first sharp bend then turn right on a cobbled path cutting out the next bend. Continuing our climb along the track, we pass a junction beside a house with large green gates (Wp.5 130M) and start descending. A gentle downhill stroll along a reddish dirt track brings us through a green gate into countryside so peaceful it's hard to believe its flanked by two busy tourist resorts. The only jarring sights are the new buildings creeping up the headland above **Port de Sóller** and, just ahead of us, a bright orange house flying six vivid flags - belonging to an association of artists, 'un poco especial' according to locals!

After the slightly dilapidated **Can Alfonso** (orange juice and locally produced jam for sale), we bear left at a Y-junction, go through another gate, and climb past **Son Llampalles**, distinguished largely by tiny bulldozers and a mini-sawmill. The dirt track levels out before climbing past **Can Carol** and **Can Bernat**, after which we descend to rejoin our outward route (Wp.6 150M) a little way above **Es Figueral**, twenty-five minutes from the start.

If you want to take the Son Llampalles dirt track from Port de Sóller, It is the concrete track on the right at km 3.2 of the PMV-2124 (just after the entrance to **Es Bosc**).

10 THREE VILLAGES + ONE THUNDERING GREAT CLIMB

Essentially, this itinerary is two loops tacked onto one another and can easily be broken into several smaller walks. The basic loop is the classic tour from **Sóller** of **Binibassi**, **Fornalutx** and **Biniaraix**, a lovely, bucolic stroll that should be within everyone's range. On top of that, the energetic have the option of climbing a superb donkey trail to **Sa Bassa** and the **Mirador de ses Barques**, from where another donkey trail brings us back to **Fornalutx**.

4* (4H) ** ⟹ 14 km ⋀ 500m / 500m ↻ 🍴 5

*Short Versions (a) 4, (b) 2   **Short Versions (a) 3hours, (b) 1½ hours

Short Versions (a) from **Fornalutx** cutting the tour of the villages (b) taxi/bus to km43 of the C-710 and descend to **Fornalutx**	Stroll the three villages	Extensions see Walks 9, 12 & 13

Access: on foot from **Sóller**

From **Sóller's** central **Plaza de sa Constitució**, we take **Carrer de sa Lluna** next to the BBVA bank, then turn second left on **Carrer de la Victoria 11 Maig**.

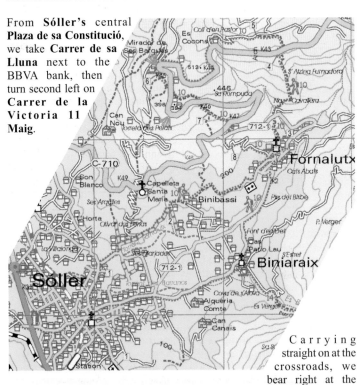

Carrying straight on at the crossroads, we bear right at the bridge (signposted 'Piscina Municipal') into **Avenguda d'Asturies**, then turn right at the football field on the **Biniaraix/Fornalutx** road (Wp.1 10M).

When the road crosses **Pont de Can Rave**, we turn left on a tarmac lane (signposted 'Fornalutx'), which promptly swings right, passing two signposted branches (see Walk 12). Bearing left at the end of the lane (Wp.2 25M), we climb a partially cobbled trail to the idyllic hamlet of **Binibassi**. Ignoring the access road, we bear left (signposted 'Fornalutx') beside a trough-like culvert to take the footpath out of the hamlet.

After going through a green gate, we follow a broad trail across terraces before bearing right at a waypost to take a narrow path marked with red dots. We immediately go through another gate and bear right down a stepped descent onto a path running alongside a high retaining wall. The path leads onto a tarmac and concrete lane passing terraces dotted with sheep and dwarf ponies. The lane dips then climbs past the **Fornalutx** cemetery before leading into the village itself (45M). Ignoring the road descending to the right, we continue straight ahead, passing the kindergarten to join **Carrer de Sol**, from where **Carrer de sa Plaza** leads into the main village square (50M). If you don't intend doing the full walk, return to **Carrer de Sol** after exploring the village.

For the full walk

We climb the steps next to **Fornalutx** church and, from **Carrer des Vent**, take **Carrer de Tramuntana** up to the **Camí de s'Alzina Fumadora / Sa Comuna** (Wp.3 55M). Climbing past hillside smallholdings, we cross the **Fornalutx** access road, where we pass above a small fenced reservoir and take a concrete track, 30 metres along which, a signpost indicates our donkey trail on the left.

For the next half-hour, we simply follow the cobbled trail, if something that climbs so relentlessly can be described as 'simple'. The long, shallow steps look easy, but they're deceptively steep and there's every chance you'll reach the top wishing never to see another step again.

Camí de s'Alzina Fumadora

However, the effort is amply rewarded with superb views across the intricate jigsaw of terraces climbing towards the **Ofre** ridge to the south. After crossing an access track, we climb steadily to go through a wire gate. The climb gets even steeper, passing a waypost and zigzagging up across terraces, before finally emerging on the C-710, just east of km 43 at a signpost for 'Fornalutx 45M' (Wp.4 90M).

Fifty metres to the right, we take a signposted path ('Pla de sa Bassa') crossing a stile then a *sitja*, where the path broadens to a trail climbing to join a rough dirt track behind a green fire-fighting reservoir (Wp.5 105M). Turning left, we follow the track round the base of **Sa Bassa**, going through the natural gateway of **Coll d'en Pastor**, before descending through rubble strewn switchbacks to one of the **Es Cocons** access gates. We bear left, down to a second gate, possibly locked but an easy climb over the left hand pillar, onto the C-710 at km 43.7.

Unfortunately, we now have over a kilometre on the road to descend to the **Mirador de ses Barques**. At the *mirador* car park, we cross onto the right hand side of the road and, as the road bears left, go through the gap between the stone and metal crash barriers (Wp.6 140M), just behind which a signpost indicates the common start of the **Sóller/Fornalutx/Port de Sóller** paths.

After descending along a narrow path with a steel cable handrail, we go through a bedstead gate and turn left to rejoin the C-710 100 metres later. 150 metres along the road, we bear left on a dirt track signposted 'Fornalutx/Costa d'en Nico'. The track passes two houses before being blocked by a gate, where we turn right to join the cobbled donkey trail down to **Fornalutx**. The first narrow stretch descends directly to the road. 50 metres to the left, we take a signposted concrete track for 10 metres until a waypoint indicates the next stage of the donkey trail descending to our left. Taking care not to drift off onto the terraces, we follow the donkey trail until it runs into a broader stony track (Wp.7 170M). We bear left for 30 metres before branching right on cobbled steps to cut out a bend. 50 metres further along the track, another section of donkey trail cuts out a second bend, after which the track descends to cross the C-710 (173M) for the last time.

On the other side of the road, we follow a concrete driveway behind a house then cross the gravelled area in front of a carport. We then cross the **Fornalutx** access road onto a tarmac lane, which we follow till a waypost (Wp.8 180M) indicates a shortcut avoiding a bend. We now repeat this procedure, following and crossing the lane five times. Behind the first house on the outskirts of **Fornalutx**, we leave the lane and take the steps behind the house down to **Carrer de la Pau**. Bearing left we come back to **Carrer de Sol**.

To return to Sóller from Fornalutx
We turn right on **Carrer de Sol** and descend to the main road in front of the principal **Fornalutx** car-park. Bearing right, we follow the road past the **Per Amunt Restaurant**, then bear left on **Carrer Mallorca** (signposted 'Sóller a Peu'), cutting a bend in the road. After a second shortcut lane, we follow the road for 500 metres, taking the second turning on the left, a narrow lane that brings us into **Biniaraix** (210M). Turning right on the **Carrer de Sant Josep**, we walk through the small square in front of the Bar/Bodega and follow the 'Sóller a Peu' signs before steps lead down to the road, which we follow back to **Sóller** (225M). Ignoring traffic signs suggesting the town centre is on our right (it ain't), we carry straight on to rejoin **Carrer de sa Lluna**.

11 THE ULTIMATE PICNIC WALK: TORRE PICADA & SA ILLETA

This is the ultimate picnic walk, climbing to the **Torre Picada** watchtower above **Port de Sóller** for coffee and biscuits, then following a lovely corniche path to a *sitja* below the **Puig Balitx** cliffs for an aperitif, before finally descending to a superb look-out point over **Sa Illeta** island for the main picnic - come prepared! A good family walk.

* 1 (if you drive to **Coll d'es Figueral**) ** + 20 minutes for the **Punta Larga** extension

Short Version	**Extension**
Cut out either the climb to **Torre Picada** or the descent toward **Sa Illeta**.	It is possible to continue from Wp.7 to the **Coll de Cordellina**, joining old routes over **Puig Balitx** and into the **Balitx** valley, but it's not recommended. There are two slightly 'delicate' passages en route to the *coll*, after which pathfinding is a problem.
	The only recommended extension is a descent to the **Punta Larga** inlet for a swim.

Access: on foot from **Port de Sóller**.

From **Port de Sóller** sea front, we take the road between the **Hotel Generoso** and the dry stream (Wp.1 0M) into **Avenguida 11 de Maig** and **Carrer de Belgica**. After a steady climb, the road swings sharp left (Wp.2 10M) and we maintain direction on a narrow tarmac lane. The lane climbs steadily then steeply between olive terraces before bearing right in front of a concrete pillar gateway, beyond which there's a small parking area beyond which there's a flat area of beaten earth pricked by the stubby heads of two metal ventilation chimneys (**Coll d'es Figueral**, Wp.3 20M). For our coffee break at the *torre*, we go through the gateway and immediately turn left onto the red-waymarked path between the trees.

The path climbs gently, passing several shortcuts, before emerging on a dirt track just below a T-junction backed by mounds of rubble. Taking the right hand branch of the T, we climb the broad track till it dwindles to a trail leading to the **Torre Picada** (Wp.4 30M) from where we have fine views along the coast and inland. On the nearside of the tower, a trodden path leads down to a grassy platform that's ideal for our coffee break. To return to the *coll*, we retrace our steps and, 75 metres after the stone gateway to the tower, where the trail widens to a track under the pines, bear left on a narrow, waymarked path. Rejoining the main track lower down, we bear left again and follow the track back to the *coll* (40M).

We now continue along the tarmac lane, which soon levels out, bringing us into fine views of the **Penyal Bernat** pinnacle and **Sa Illeta**, and passing a sign for 'Es Coll des Ille, Privat', shortly after which the tarmac ends and we

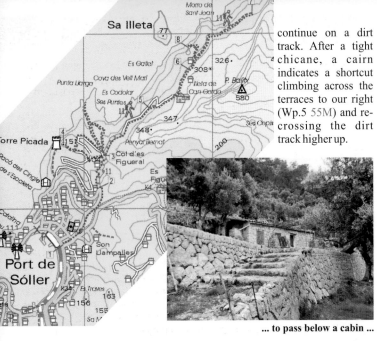

continue on a dirt track. After a tight chicane, a cairn indicates a shortcut climbing across the terraces to our right (Wp.5 55M) and re-crossing the dirt track higher up.

... to pass below a cabin ...

At the second junction with the dirt track, we bear left to pass below a cabin. We now continue along the dirt track, passing the idyllically situated and well-restored main house and several satellite cabins. Shortly after passing the drive to **Can Bardi**, we come to a locked green gate where cairns to the right indicate a way through the fence above the gate (Wp.6 70M).

We then walk along a retaining wall for 20 metres and, ignoring the main trail that continues through a wall-gate with a stone hinge bracket, bear left to descend through another gap in the wall, just after which there's a Y-junction of paths. The branch on the left is the way down to our picnic spot, but for the moment we continue on the main path, descending gently through the woods. The path comes into fine views of the cliffs below **Es Joncar** and passes a slightly vertiginous stretch before ending in a *sitja* (Wp.7 90M), just in time for an aperitif. (N.B. The waymarked routes continuing from this *sitja* both involve some precarious scrambling and are <u>not</u> recommended.)

Refreshed by our aperitif, we retrace our steps to the branch path just after Wp.6 and take the lower path descending steadily on a slippery carpet of pine needles to a stand of half-a-dozen water barrels fed by a spring (Wp.8 125M). After eating our fill and gazing on the great crocodile's snout of **Sa Illeta**, where hundreds of seagulls swirl overhead like swarms of midges, we return by the same route.

If you want to bathe on the way back, take the narrow path descending north from **Coll d'es Figueral**. (It's possible to make a loop using the broad track heading NE, but this doesn't add much and is only recommended for those wishing to while away an afternoon exploring the headland). When the path comes into a slight rise, soon blocked by fallen pine, bear left and follow the gully down to a lovely little inlet, ideal for rock-bathing in calm seas.

This pleasant short walk follows two classic cobbled trails climbing towards the **Mirador de ses Barques**. Despite recent wayposting, these routes are little used nowadays, which is a pity as they provide a perfect introduction to the peaceful countryside around **Sóller**.

2	1H 40M	6 km	230m 230m	0 *

Extension	Stroll	*3, if doing the extension
To the **Mirador de ses Barques** and **Port de Sóller** (see Walk 13)	To the Chapel (Wp.2), returning via the dirt track	

Access: on foot from **Sóller**

We start as per Walk 10, following the **Fornalutx** road past the football field and turning left at the **Pont de Can Rave**. Ignoring the concrete track 150 metres later (**Camí de ses Marjades**), we turn left 50 metres further along onto the **Camí de sa Capelleta** (Wp.1 15M). The path climbs behind two houses and crosses a dirt track. At a second junction with the track, we bear right and, 100 metres later, turn left to recover the path.

Capelleta de Santa María We then cross the track three more times before joining the final stepped ascent (briefly interrupted by the track) to the **Capelleta de Santa Maria** (Wp.2 27M).The chapel is a nicely proportioned building and benches outside provide a pleasant spot for a breather, though the interior is chiefly remarkable for its egg-box wall (NOT a metaphor!).

Continuing our ascent from the chapel gates, we cross the C-710 onto a clear well-marked path that climbs steadily, occasionally alongside, occasionally crossing a concrete track before joining the **Costa d'en Flassada** path (Wp.3 35M).

Bearing right, we continue climbing between terraces, coming into fine views of the **Mitx Dia** on our right.

At the next junction with the concrete track, we bear right to recover the wayposted path 30 metres later. Steady climbing brings us to another signposted concrete track (Wp.4 45M) where we join the descent of Walk 13. Bearing left (in the direction of **Port de Sóller**), we contour round the mountain, following the track as the concrete gives way to dirt. After 500 metres, the track swings right, climbing through another concreted section (Wp.5 55M).

or the **Mirador de ses Barques**, bear right and follow the waymarked walking trail visible just above us (Walk 13 Wp.2). For **Port de Sóller**, bear right and stay on the track. Otherwise, turn left to descend the initially grassy then cobbled path between terraces.

After going through a gate and passing a small spring, the path runs into a track descending to a large farmhouse (**Can Nou**), just below which we bear left, off the tarmac driveway, onto a grassy path marked by blue arrows (Wp.6 65M). Going through a light wire-mesh gate, we recover the cobbled trail and cross more terraces. After a sturdier metal gate, we continue our steady descent down to the C-710.

Crossing the road, we take the concrete driveway down to **Can Bisbal**, where a final cobbled stretch leads into a concrete and tarmac lane (**Camí Vell de Balitx**), which ends at a T-junction with the **Camí de Son Blanco**. We turn right at the T-junction, then left at the next T-junction and follow the **Camí de ses Argiles** back past the football ground and into **Sóller**, as per Walk 9.

This attractive, little known link between the **Coll d'en Marques** and the **Mirador de ses Barques** is a very versatile itinerary, serving as a short walk in itself, an alternative path to **Sóller** (see Walk 12 Wp.5), and a way into the **Balitx Valley** and onto the popular one-way route to **Cala Tuent**.

* (U - see 'Timings' on page 9) + 1¼h if climbing from **Port de Sóller**
** + 55M for **Balitx d'en Mig** OR 1h 40 for **Balitx d'Avall**
*** + 300 metres for the extension

Access: by car or on foot from **Port de Sóller**. There's parking for two small cars on the northern side of the **Coll d'en Marques**.

Extension	Stroll
Balitx Valley (see text)	From the **Mirador de ses Barques**, take the dirt track (N) to join the walk at Wp. 4

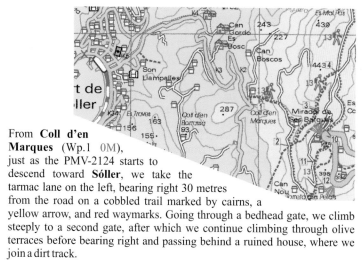

From **Coll d'en Marques** (Wp.1 0M), just as the PMV-2124 starts to descend toward **Sóller**, we take the tarmac lane on the left, bearing right 30 metres from the road on a cobbled trail marked by cairns, a yellow arrow, and red waymarks. Going through a bedhead gate, we climb steeply to a second gate, after which we continue climbing through olive terraces before bearing right and passing behind a ruined house, where we join a dirt track.

Bearing left on the dirt track, we climb towards a new house, just before which we turn right onto a path marked with cairns and waymarks. Fifty metres along this path, we go through a wooden-frame gate under the natural arch of a carob tree, beyond which we walk between crumbling retaining walls, initially on the level, then climbing slightly at a point where a steel cable has been set in the rock as a handrail.

Thirty metres later, we go through a bedstead gate to join a dirt track next to a small concrete cabin. Maintaining direction (SE) we follow the track behind the cabin, going through two green gates, the second next to an old farmhouse. The track then descends through a concreted bend before winding along the contour line to a second concreted bend (Wp.2 25M), where we turn left, leaving the track to take a broad cobbled path marked with cairns, blue arrows and red waymarks that guide us up past terraces.

At the <u>second</u> large <u>metal</u> gate, we ignore a branch to the right and maintain direction (N) following the blue arrows to join a dirt track (Wp.3 35M) 200 metres north-west of the *mirador*. We bear left along the track for a few metres (<u>away</u> from the *mirador*) to recover the blue and yellow waymarked path. The path goes through a bedstead gate onto a cobbled stretch climbing through neatly terraced olive groves onto a broad *coll* where it joins the dirt track from the *mirador* (Wp.4 45M) next to a signpost ('Sóller/Fornalutx/Mirador de ses Barques'). You could take the *mirador* path straight away, but I recommend following the extension at least as far as **Balitx d'en Mig**.

Extension
Turning left we stroll along the dirt track, passing a 'Tuent/Sa Calobra' signpost (Wp.5 10M from Wp.4) in front of the **Balitx de Dalt** farmhouse. Continuing through the green gates on the main track, we come into splendid views of the **Balitx Valley**. 200 metres later, we leave the track at a waypost (Wp.6 15M) to take a cobbled trail down to **Font de Balitx**. Ignoring a path on the right, we turn left and follow the intermittently cobbled path down to rejoin the dirt track near the ruined **Balitx d'en Mig** farmhouse (Wp.7 25M).

Unless you intend going all the way to **Cala Tuent** or are really desperate for an orange juice, I suggest turning back here, taking the dirt track back to Wp.4 (N.B. Ignore a branch at the first left hand bend 200 metres from **Balitx d'en Mig**) in a little under thirty minutes.

To continue to Balitx d'Avall
We follow the main track down to a junction in front of a new house, where a signpost (Wp.8 35M from Wp.4) indicates a cobbled trail descending to rejoin the track (Wp.9 45M) 50 metres above the **Balitx d'Avall** farmhouse, where fresh orange juice is available. From here, it takes a little under an hour following the main dirt track (NE) to cross the **Coll de Biniamar** and join Walk 21 to **Cala Tuent**. For today though, we return by the dirt track back to the *coll* at Wp.4 (roughly 50M from **Balitx d'Avall**).

To reach the Mirador de ses Barques from Wp.4
We could simply follow the dirt track, but it's nicer to take the signposted, waymarked path. A gentle climb brings us through a green gate, after which a clear level path leads between weekend *casetas* before broadening to a dirt track. After crossing a small rise and arriving at the top of a concreted section, we leave the track, bearing right on a blue-waymarked path down to the *mirador* (Wp.10 55M excluding the extension).

The path to Mirador de ses Barques.

Crossing the *mirador* car-park, we take the signposted path for 'Fornalutx/Port Sóller'. After passing a stretch with a steel cable handrail, we descend through a gate to a second signpost indicating branches for 'Fornalutx' and 'Sóller'. We follow 'Sóller', descending steadily through a lovely natural tunnel formed by a deeply embedded cobbled path and a high canopy of oak trees to join a stony track (Wp.11 65M). Bearing left, we pass a gate topped with the metal letters '**Es Figueral**', 100 metres after which, we leave the track (Wp.12 70M) and take the blue waymarked path below the house on the left.

Descending across terraces, we emerge on a dirt track signposted 'Tuent/Sa Costera'. Turning left and immediately right, we join a concrete track, 10 metres along which another signpost indicates 'Port Sóller' to the right. After passing the entrance to **Ses Moncades**, the concrete deteriorates and eventually gives way to dirt.

The track winds along the contour and climbs slightly to a sharp right hand bend where it is concreted again. Ignoring the waymarked path on the left, we climb the concrete to rejoin our outward route at Wp.2 (85M), twenty minutes from our starting point.

This itinerary is well known and a bit of a motorway, but not without reason: easy walking, great views, a lovely 'high mountain' feel on the **Cúber** plain, and a spectacular descent make this one of the classics. You may question the Exertion Rating given the descent, but it's so easily staged along a beautifully cobbled donkey track, I can almost guarantee your knees won't notice it. Do wear good footwear, though. The cobbles can be murder on inadequately shod feet.

| 2 | 3H * | 12 km | 120m / 900m | ⇔ | 5 ** |

| * Short Version 2h | **Stroll** | **Short Version** |
| ** in **Biniaraix** (if you don't mind paying €4 for an orange juice - you probably won't). | For a pleasant picnic spot, from **Biniaraix** to the second bridge and back. | For the views, to the **Coll de l'Ofre** and back. |

Access: by bus (in season), taxi (€20 from **Sóller**), and car (Short Version) to km34 of the C-710.

From the parking area at the **Cúber Reservoir** (Wp.1 0M), we take the tarmac track alongside the reservoir and cross the dam wall to follow a dirt track past the refuge/*área recreativa*.

A pleasant twenty-five minute stroll leads to the **Ofre** estate, where we are greeted by a sign warning of bulls: don't panic - given the number of hiking parties that come trundling through here, I imagine any

Cúber Reservoir

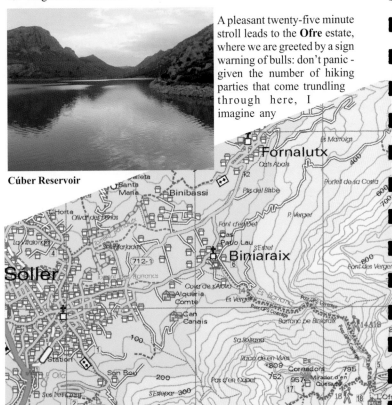

sane bull would flee at the merest suggestion of a rambler. Shortly after passing a house (unmarked on most maps and unnameable according to the locals!), the track swings left and we bear right on a GR-signposted path into the woods (Wp.2 50M). A gentle climb through the woods along a clear path brings us back onto the dirt track (Wp.3 60M) at the **Coll de l'Ofre** beside another GR-signpost.

Fifty metres later, we leave the dirt track and bear right on a wayposted path through a wall gateway. Rejoining the dirt track after 75 metres, we immediately turn right onto another wayposted path. Descending gently through the woods, we cross the dirt track again and descend steadily to a T-junction (Wp.4 75M), where we turn right then left when we rejoin the dirt track. Descending past a telescope, we turn right on another signposted path (Wp.5 85M) as the track bears round to **Ofre** farmhouse. One hundred metres later we go through a green gate into the **Barranc de Biniaraix**, where we join a cobbled donkey trail and what has been a pleasant walk becomes spectacular.

The trail descends alongside the **Biniaraix** torrent before levelling out above cliff tops, from where we have superb views down to **Sóller** and the sea. Leaving the **Ofre** estate by another green gate, we resume our descent below towering cliffs streaked with water stains. We cross the torrent three times, after which it dries out and we continue our steady descent through shady, green terraces. After a fourth crossing, a very gentle climb brings us onto a dirt track leading into **Biniaraix** beside the old *lavadero* (Wp.6 155M). Bearing left through the village, we pass (or possibly not) the enticing but expensive Bar/Bodega, and follow the road for fifteen minutes down to **Sóller**.

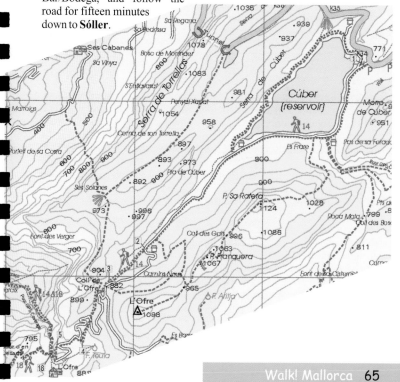

15 SA RATETA & L'OFRE

L'Ofre is the distinctive conical peak south-east of **Sóller** that, from a distance, seems to be mantled in a dense cloak of trees except for a small tonsure on top. **Sa Rateta**, considerably less celebrated than its august neighbour, is the scruffy little summit south of the **Cúber Reservoir**. For my money though, the latter is a far more satisfying climb. **L'Ofre** is such a classic it's elbow room only on a busy day, whereas the wild pathless approach to **Sa Rateta** guarantees space for the most angular joints, and the views are as good if not better. Hence **L'Ofre** is merely an extension to my main loop. However, this is a rough, pathless route, only recommended for experienced walkers. There are at least three points when you think, 'It's not possible, that *can't* be the way!'

5*	3½ H **** *****	10.5 km	↗ 450m **** ↘ 450m	↻	0

* just – it's no great climb, but the rough terrain is testing
** + ½h for the extension   ***Short Version 2½ h return
**** + 150 metres for L'Ofre

Short Version	**Stroll**
For an easier ascent of **L'Ofre**, follow the walk in reverse and climb from Wp.12. The byre mentioned in the text is the first building on the right (excluding a roofless ruin) after the *peligro toros*, 'danger bulls' sign, 15M from the **Ofre** gates.	As per the Short Version, but stopping to picnic beneath the poplars above Wp.12.
	Extension
	L'Ofre (see text). Walk 14 could also be incorporated with this route.

Access: by car or bus (seasonal timetable)

From the **Cúber** parking area (Wp.1 0M), we take the tarmac track alongside the reservoir. As the track curves left, look up to the left of the dam wall for a narrow scree gully climbing steeply to a small ridge and large pine tree, beyond which is a shallow valley. Our itinerary joins the scree gully at the bend and climbs along the upper half into the valley behind the pine. One look will tell you this is impossible, but have faith – it will already look marginally more possible from the dam wall. Between the dam wall and the small quarry on its right, there's a sloping outcrop of rock. We have to cross that outcrop and the *carritx* covered slope to its left, to reach the scree-filled gully.

Forty metres after crossing the dam wall, we leave the dirt track just before a stubby concrete post (Wp.2 10M). Crossing a patch of grass, we climb (S) onto the sloping outcrop of rock through a small but obvious channel muddied by previous pedestrians - possibly sheep, but they knew what they were doing! Picking our way across the rocks and through the *carritx*, we gradually climb to the right, bringing the pine tree at the head of the gully into clearer focus. After traversing the sloping outcrop (20M), we continue climbing across the *carritx* covered slope, which is in fact quite a large valley. Joining a cairn-marked route coming from the west, we aim for the two bushier holm oak between us and the gully (SSE). Passing behind the two bushier oak, we find a large cairn and, after a short, rocky climb to a sorrier looking oak, bear left on a more or less level stretch to reach the remains of a wall flanking the scree filled gully (Wp.3 30M).

Maintaining direction (ESE) we follow a faint trodden way through the *carritx* above the scree to the head of the gully, where a final steep climb (take care to follow the cairns) leads up to the large pine tree (Wp.4 40M). We now follow the cairns into the shallow valley, which is not quite so shallow once you're in it. On entering the valley, we turn right and follow the steep cairn-marked route up the rocks, sticking to the smoother flanking rocks rather than the debris in the middle, except briefly, 200 metres from the visible top, where we dip into the valley before swinging back to the rocks on the right.

We emerge on a rough limestone plateau (Wp.5 70M) behind **Sa Rateta**, which is clearly visible.

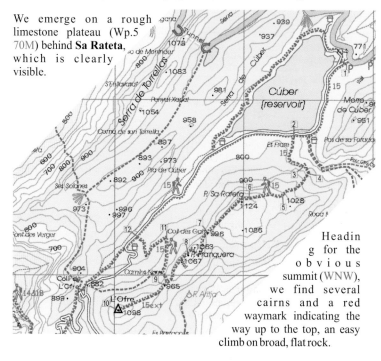

Heading for the obvious summit (WNW), we find several cairns and a red waymark indicating the way up to the top, an easy climb on broad, flat rock.

I recommend stopping at the first little summit (Wp.6 85M) rather than the higher one, since the views are better from here. Continuing along the ridge on broad limestone pavement, we come to a cairn marking the start of a steep stony descent to the grassy **Coll des Gats**. We can either descend directly to the *coll* (as mapped), or bear left just before the steep descent on a new, cairn-marked way. If you take the direct route, about halfway down, traces branch off in both directions - we bear left, away from the cliffs! As you descend, you'll probably be glancing at the crag beyond the *coll*, thinking, 'There's no way up there'. Again, there is. Just to the left of the crag, there is what appears to be a very shallow gully, which is our way back up onto the ridge.

Crossing the **Coll des Gats** (Wp.7 110M), we bear left 5 metres below a solitary dead tree to cross rocks and reddish earth leading to a line of cairns below a huge boulder (also visible from the far side of the *coll*). Seventy-five metres after the boulder, we go over a small rise and bear right climbing natural rock steps (SSW) for a further 30 metres before swinging sharp right to climb the 'very shallow gully' (NW), in fact more rock steps, bringing us back onto the ridge behind the crag.

Puig Major and Cúber reservoir

Bearing left and staying well back from the cliffs, which are more abrupt here, we climb to the small **Franquera** summits (Wp.8 130M). The limestone is rougher and more fractured, but it's still relatively easy walking as we head for a wall, only the top of which is visible at first, making it look like a cabin. Crossing the wall 15 metres from its upper end, we descend (SW) along another steep, stony way down to the unnamed *coll* above **Camins Nou** (Wp.9 145M).

Extension

Climbing onto the rocks to the left of the pylon, we follow the cairns up to **L'Ofre**. The path seems clear, but follow the cairns carefully, as there are a maze of paths shortly after the *coll*. We finally join the main waymarked route just below the peak, from where we follow the blue arrows up across the rocks to the top (Wp.10 15M from Wp.9).

To return to Cúber from Wp.9

Bearing north, we cross a broken wall to take a clear path down to a Y-junction. Continuing straight on (the right hand branch), we bear right at the next metal pylon and descend steadily through the pine, passing occasional cairns before emerging at a large *sitja* (Wp.11 155M [excluding the extension]). We bear left (SW) on a broad trail descending to a trickling stream and large trough next to a fine stand of poplars. Taking the fainter of the two cow paths on the eastern side of the stream, we meander down in a most inconsequential and cow-like fashion, crossing a tangle of paths, half-paths and watershed channels, to emerge on the **Ofre** dirt track opposite a small byre (Wp.12 170M). Turning right, we follow the dirt track back to our starting point.

16 TOSSALS VERDS CIRCUIT

This adventurous excursion takes us through five rough tunnels piping water down from the **Cúber** reservoir, visits Mallorca's first manned and still most popular refuge, and circles the **Tossals Verds** massif along shady charcoal-burning paths. It is possible to cross all except the second tunnel without a torch (if you don't mind not seeing where you put your feet), but not recommended. During the descent, you will see painted signs announcing a toll for the privilege of crossing the **Solleric** estate. I have not heard of anyone actually being asked to pay.

| 4* | **4 H** | ⟹ 13 km | ⋀⋀ 450m / 450m | ↻ | 🍴 4 *** |

* Short Version **(a)** & **(b)** 3 **Short Version (a) 3h (b) 2h (estimated times)
*** The refuge (open all year) and has dormitory accommodation for 30. Book even for eating, as it's popular with large parties (Tel: 971 182027).

Short Versions	**Stroll**	**Extension**
(a) to **Cases Velles** in reverse **(b)** to the refuge from the **Almedrà** hamlet on the access road from **Lloseta** (see map)	Follow the dirt tracks circling the reservoir.	see Walk 17

Access: by car and bus.

Starting from the **Área Recreativa de Sa Font des Noguera** at km 33.8 of the C-710 (Wp.1 0M), we cross the stile at the western end of the car-park and follow the GR (signposted 'Barranc de Biniarix') round to the **Cúber Reservoir**, where we take the tarmac track along the reservoir. When the tarmac track swings right to cross the dam wall (Wp.2 10M), we bear left on a dirt track. The track soon narrows to a walking trail descending steeply on loose stones and <u>passing</u> a tunnel with a concrete pipe running through it – this is NOT one of our tunnels. Ten minutes from the dam wall we cross a torrent, then follow the course of the large, occasionally interred concrete water-pipe, along an easy dirt path. A steady then gentle climb brings us through a cutting onto a small plateau littered with sections of discarded piping.

Descending from the plateau, gently at first then more steeply along a rough, rock strewn path, we come to the first of the tunnels (on our right), dubbed 'Sollerich Paso', (Wp.3 40M).

The valley above the tunnels

The first tunnel is easy, the second less so: you can't see the exit, the ground's rough, it dips down at the end, and you have to be careful not to clout your head on the roof. After a much longer descent, we come to the third tunnel, which has a low entrance, but is in fact easier than the first two with a well beaten path and large window halfway along. The fourth is little more than an archway, the fifth and last has been roughly gated. Leaving

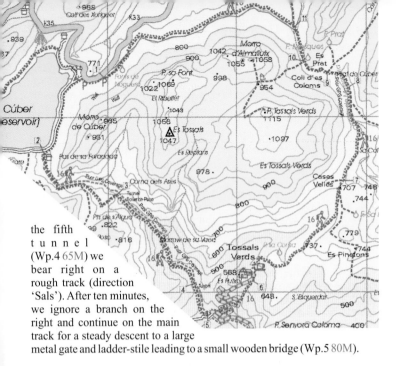

the fifth tunnel (Wp.4 65M) we bear right on a rough track (direction 'Sals'). After ten minutes, we ignore a branch on the right and continue on the main track for a steady descent to a large metal gate and ladder-stile leading to a small wooden bridge (Wp.5 80M).

Crossing the bridge, we join the tarmac lane from **Almedrà**. After climbing up the lane for ten minutes, we bear right at a signpost indicating the refuge is a further ten minutes away, and follow a stony trail climbing steeply across the terraces. We rejoin the lane shortly before the refuge gates (Wp.6 100M), from where we have good views of the **Alcaldena** and **Alaró** mountains to the south-west. To the left of the main refuge building, we take the signposted path on the right for 'Cases Velles 35M / Font des Noguera 2H', passing through a gate and climbing across terraces. A steady then gentle climb with fine views of the terraced valley below **Cases Velles**, passes first a large pine tree (to our left), **El Fumat**, reputedly the largest of its kind in the region, then a signposted path on the right for **Mancor des Valles** (not recommended). A path to the left (Wp.7 140M) a few metres before a GR waypost, leads to the terraces below **Cases Velles**, where there are innumerable fine picnic spots.

N.B. If you're doing this in reverse, the turning is on the right shortly after a sharply angled wall.

Continuing along the main path, we circle **Tossals Verds**, passing the celebrated **Canaleta de Massanella** (see Appendix D), before crossing and re-crossing the stream just below it (Wp.8 200M). A gentle climb brings us past the turning for **Massanella** and **Lluc**, signposted 'Font d'es Prat' (Wp.9 205M) and the branch to **Puig Tossals Verds** (Wp.10 210M). We then cross **Coll d'es Colloms** for a steady descent along a roughly cobbled trail down to a gate and a bridge over the new concrete *canaleta* (Wp.11 225M N.B. If doing this route in reverse, this is the fourth and broadest concrete ramped bridge over the *canaleta*, also distinguished by a GR waypost). Bearing left, we walk alongside the *canaleta* (doubtless on a hot day wishing we were IN it) back to our starting point in a little over thirty minutes.

17 TWIN PEAKS AND ONE MAD MALLORCAN LOOP

The **Tossals Verds Circuit** is well known, yet hardly anybody ventures up the massif itself, which is puzzling because it's an easy climb to a wonderful little wilderness. The **Twin Peaks** are **Puig de Tossals Verds** and **Morro d'Almallutx**. Both involve rough pathless walking, but neither are difficult and the first could be done by a moderately fit family. The loop is something else. Few obstacles daunt your average Mallorcan rambler and it sometimes seems as if, having established perfectly feasible, roundabout routes, locals look at the map, draw a straight line and say, 'Let's do it <u>that</u> way', regardless of what lies in between. The loop via **Es Ribellet** is far from being a straight line, but the mentality is the same. It's horrendous: very rough, very gruelling, very steep, very pathless! It was indicated to me by a young Mallorcan family, who seemed to think it suitable for children. Frankly, it's not suitable for most adults, let alone children. So why include it? Simply because I know there are people out there for whom the single word 'horrendous' will be enough to have them strapping on their boots and booking their tickets. Be warned though, it is only for very experienced walkers. Everybody else should settle for one of the Short Versions. Finally, given that this is wild, little visited terrain, please observe the basic and commonly ignored rules: Don't walk alone; Do tell someone where you're going. NOTE: **Coll d'es Colloms** is at Wp.3, <u>not</u> Wp.5 where most maps place it.

| 5* | 4-4½H** | 9 km | 725m *** 725m | ↻ | 0 |

*   Short Versions **(a)** & **(b)** 4
**   (U - see 'Timings' in the introduction) Short Version **(a)** 3 h **(b)** 3½ h (estimated times)
*** Short Version **(a)** 300 metres **(b)** 375 metres

Short Versions
(a) **Morro d'Almallutx** returning via **Coll d'es Colloms**
(b) **Puig Tossals Verds** returning via **Coll d'es Colloms**

Stroll
Along the *canaleta* to a huge boulder with a small oak growing from its crown.

Access: by car or bus (seasonal timetable)

Starting just below **Font des Noguera Área Recreativa**, we take the GR-212 east, signposted 'Font d'es Prat/Refugi des Tossals Verds' (Wp.1 0M), and follow the open concrete *canaleta* until it swings round into the **Almallutx** valley, where we cross the *canaleta* via a broad concrete ramp (the fourth) (Wp.2 30M). We then go through a wooden gate and climb steadily through the oak wood along a partially stepped charcoal-burners' trail that levels out on the **Coll d'es**

Morro d'Almallutx & Puig de sa Font

Colloms, from where we can see our **Twin Peaks** up to the right. 30 metres after the *coll*, a GR signpost indicates our branch on the right (Wp.3 40M) N.B. This post was decidedly unstable last time I passed. If it subsequently disappears, look for a small concrete marker stone numbered 802092.

Following a delightful sun-dappled path strewn with dead oak leaves (SSW), we pass (after 200 metres) the first of several old pink waymarks, after which the climb gradually gets steeper and the cairns larger. Bearing left at a 'Caça Controlada' signpost (Wp.4 50M), we cross the bed of a watershed, taking care to follow the cairns and waymarks, and gradually climb away from the **Morro d'Almallutx** before emerging from the oak wood behind a large pinnacle. A final brief climb along a clear, eroded path brings us through a gap in a wall (Wp.5 60M) onto the misnamed *coll* between our **Twin Peaks**. On the far side of the *coll* there is a large snowpit. We now have a choice of routes. **Tossals Verds** is the easier, gentler and less hazardous climb, despite being slightly higher, while **Morro d'Almallutx** is a rougher, wilder place, better suited to those with a passion for getting off the beaten track - though that's a passion that will be utterly sated if you do the full circuit! N.B. All subsequent timings assume climbing both peaks, though one will probably be enough for most people.

For the Morro d'Almallutx
We bear right to the ruins of the snow-gatherers' cabin, behind which a cairn marks the start of the ascent up a shallow gully. At the top of the gully, we bear left for 10 metres before swinging back to resume our northerly direction, picking our way over the rocks and passing occasional cairns indicating a rough line to the top (Wp.6 80M), where the 'Grup Es Voltors' left their mark in 1994. Taking particular care on the sharp rocks at the top, we return to Wp.5 via the same route.

For Puig d'es Tossals Verds
We bear left just before the snowpit on the *coll*, and climb along a reasonably clear way marked with cairns, heading for the rocky outcrop to the right of the *puig* (SSW). A steady climb with fine views of **Puig Major** leads to a large cairn (Wp.7 110M) 50 metres behind the guiding outcrop, in full view of the **Alaró** and **Alcaldena** 'sugar loaf' mountains. Bearing left, we follow the clear, cairn-marked way (NE) up to the **Tossals Verds** trig point (Wp.8 120M). We return to Wp.5 via the same route.

This is probably enough mountain for most people and I recommend returning to **Font d'es Noguera via Coll d'es Colloms**. If you feel like an adventure though, head west. But remember: this is pathless country with steep descents and only sporadic cairns to help us on our way.

For the full circuit (EXT)
We head into the valley to the west of the snowpit and follow the cairn marked route, meandering through the *carritx* then dipping down to pass below two huge fingers of rock poking out from the northern ridge (Wp.9 145M [7M from the *coll*]). Bearing right (NW), we follow cairns up to a depression in the ridge to the right of a small top flanked by a pinnacle of rock. Turning towards the pinnacle, we skirt the first small top (SW) to cross onto a second depression in the ridge with superb views over **Gorg Blau** (Wp.10 155M).

We now follow the ridge (W) staying a little way behind the crest and passing

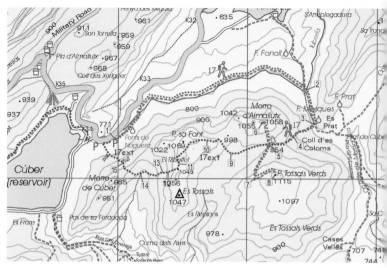

very occasional cairns. Staying below the jagged limestone running up to **Puig de sa Font** (barely distinguishable from the rest of the ridge), we pick our way through *carritx* (SW) toward two distinct small tops on our left (S), the second of which, **Es Tossals**, has a large, clearly visible cairn on top. Just before the first of these two tops, with the **Cúber** reservoir visible to the north-west, a cairn (Wp.11 175M) marks the start of our first <u>very rough</u> descent. If you look to the right, you'll see a wall along a narrow ridge with a path snaking up to the wall from the south. This path is our objective.

There's no approved way down to this path, only a steep scree slope, and it's basically a question of picking your way down as best you can. Walking poles may be useful, otherwise you have to grab the *carritx* and whatever comes to hand to steady yourself on the steeper sections. It's slightly easier if you hug the rocks on the left until about 50 metres before they end in a large knoll. From here, we bear right, away from the rocks to cut across into the main channel of scree, where we find another cairn (Wp.12 190M). We now take maximum advantage of every potential zigzag, passing two more cairns on a long chute of debris (Wp.13 200M) and aiming for the obvious v-shaped defile at the bottom of the slope. Finally, with considerable relief, we lever ourselves down the defile and cross the remaining 75 metres of scrub and rock to join the path (Wp.14 210M) above the orange and white wreck of a light aircraft, visible through much of the descent.

Bearing right, we climb (sorry about this, but there's no logic to Mallorcan mountains) along the stony path to a gap in the wall on the ridge (Wp.15 220M). Winding through the rocks on the far side of the wall, we soon see the **Font des Noguera Área Recreativa** below us. Heading towards **Cúber** (NW) we pick our way through the *carritx* to a second wall, where a very rough path descends steeply to the GR-212 between the **Cúber** and **Font d'es Noguera** parking areas in a little under twenty minutes.

Very long, very high, very tough. So what's the attraction? Basically that - it's very long, very high and very tough. This is challenge time, the macho end of walking, for the sort of people who gaze at towering cliffs and say to themselves, 'I want to be up there'. If you have to ask yourself 'Can I do it?', the answer is probably no. Nonetheless, the reasons for trying aren't all childish. It is a very satisfying route, the views are unparalleled, and the ridge, which dominates the **Sóller** valley, is bound to draw the walker's eye as it's such an obvious and, in many ways, perfect loop. But I can't emphasise enough, this is <u>very tough</u> walking. Most walkers will have an idea what a 1000 metre climb entails. The difference here is that the tough walking only begins <u>after</u> you've done the climbing. Once on top, you've got four kilometres of virtually pathless terrain, hopping across fissured slabs of limestone and *carritx* covered boulders. Every step of the way is a potential twisted ankle and, since the only company you'll find on top are eagles and vultures, it's essential that you don't go alone. Thanks to the cluster of antennae above **Sa Serra**, there is some mobile phone coverage, but as ever in the mountains, this should not be relied on. And do not venture up here in poor conditions. Trackless limestone, high cliffs, deep potholes and dense cloud cover are not a happy combination. Bear in mind that conditions at this altitude and proximity to the sea can change rapidly. Twenty minutes after we descended from the ridge under clear, blue skies, it was submerged in cloud! If you're still reading, if there's a fervid gleam in your eye, if your hands are trembling and your legs twitching with excitement, then this might be the walk for you. But do observe all the usual precautions, and take plenty of food and a <u>minimum</u> of two litres water per person. The route is waymarked with red dots and cairns till Wp.8, after which we're on our own, except for a few cairns along the ridge.

*   - though distance and the roughness of the terrain send it off the scale.
** Timing is exact, but the rough terrain and pathfinding problems mean this is a more approximate guide than usual. Allow 10 h including rest-stops etc..

Short Versions & Strolls

Given the steep climb, there's little here that could be called a 'stroll', but Wps.2, 3, 4, & 6 are pleasant picnic spots and would serve as natural objectives for linear walks. Those who don't fancy the pathless ridge but want comparable views can continue along the dirt track from Wp.9 to the private **Jovenolles** refuge (see map) some twenty-five minutes to the east (visible from the **Sa Serra** farm) and return the same way.

Access: on foot from **Sóller**

From **Sóller**'s central *plaza*, we take **Carrer de Joan Baptista Ensenyat** to the left of the church. Turning first left (**Carrer de Sant Jaume**) then first right brings us into the short **Carrer de Sant Nicolau** (signposted 'Cementiri'). We turn left at the end of **Carrer de Sant Nicolau**, then right 15 metres later into **Carrer de Pau Noguera**, which we follow to the cemetery

(Wp.1 10M). Continuing on the tarmac lane past the cemetery, we ignore a path and dirt track on the right, and a concrete track on the left. 150 metres after crossing a small bridge, we leave the lane, turning left on cobbled stairs marked with red dots. The stairs climb steeply before winding through a chicane and leading into a partially cobbled path zigzagging up across abandoned terraces and passing a ruined cabin.

After climbing steadily, the path levels out briefly (Wp.2 30M) and we bear left, heading for a second ruin 15 metres away, where we climb onto a path <u>behind</u> the ruin. Climbing steadily then more steeply, we cross a second level stretch of about 50 metres, at the end of which we branch left to continue climbing, passing a partially restored cabin, **Can Selles** (Wp.3 45M), and another cabin where someone has etched Sóller's coat of arms into a rock (Wp.4 60M). After a third level stretch, from where we can glimpse the roundabout at the southern end of the **Sóller** by-pass, we come to the upper limit of the terracing. Entering a mixed pine and oak wood, the path swings left, zigzagging steeply up beside a stone wall. The route's not always clear, but it's well waymarked with red dots and, in spring, studded with tiny begonias. After a shady climb between pine, oak and tumbledown outcrops of limestone, we pass through a wall gateway (Wp.5 80M) where we bear left to continue zigzagging up through the woods (SSW).

After emerging on a level, less densely wooded, *carritx* covered ridge overlooking the steeply scarped **Rafel de Gaspar** valley on our left (E), we go through another wall gateway, beyond which we must take particular care following the waymarks through the *carritx*. 100 metres after the wall, we bear right, into the woods rather than left towards **Es Rafel**, staying more or less on the level for 50 metres before cairns indicate a path to the left. The path winds onto a natural 'terrace', climbing slightly (WSW) before swinging left to cross a dead pine with two cairns perched on the trunk. Following the cairns and waymarks, we climb steeply, sometimes on a vague path, sometimes on exposed rock, passing above a small *sitja* (Wp.6 105M).

After climbing steeply on a long limestone slope, the path bears back towards **Es Rafel** (SE), where we ignore a large cairn to the left (Wp.7 110M) and continue climbing. 50 metres later, we come onto another limestone shelf, where some cairns appear to lead us off to the left, but we in fact carry on climbing over the rocks for our first sight of the radio masts above **Sa Serra** (115M).

The path is unclear, but aiming for the tall, solitary, central antenna, we soon pick up cairns and waymarks, guiding us along what is in effect a huge spur, from where we have fine views of **Puig Major** and the **Teix Massif**. The antennae disappear behind a succession of low crags separating us from the **Sa Serra** farmhouse. Using a couple of short retaining walls, we climb behind the first crag before skirting to the left of the second and third crags. Cairns and red waymarks guide us over the final rocks, gradually

... fine views of Puig Major ...

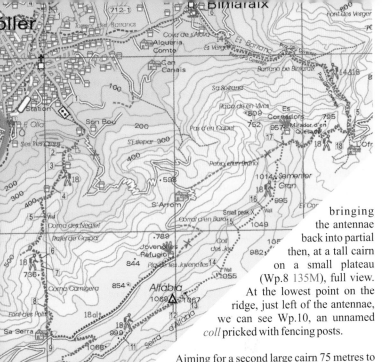

bringing the antennae back into partial then, at a tall cairn on a small plateau (Wp.8 135M), full view. At the lowest point on the ridge, just left of the antennae, we can see Wp.10, an unnamed *coll* pricked with fencing posts.

Aiming for a second large cairn 75 metres to the south then bearing left toward two smaller cairns, we pick up an old cow path on the left of the last rocky outcrop before the farm. Going through a gateway formed by the remains of an old fence and wall, we bear right (SW) to climb toward a comparatively large oak tree with distinctively tangled branches. Maintaining direction on a naturally 'cobbled' route, we come into view of the farm buildings, where the waymarks end. Going to the left of the farm, we find a clear path leading to the farm's access track (Wp.9 150M), from where we can see the roof of the **Jovenolles** refuge in the distance.

We turn left and follow the dirt track past a large pine to cross the watershed running down from the *coll*, immediately after which, we turn right, leaving the track and climbing a faint stony path for 50 metres to join the remains of an old cart track (visible as we approach the pine tree, but not from where we leave the main track) carpeted with euphorbia. The cart track climbs steadily (E) before doubling back towards the antennae (SW), re-crossing the watershed and climbing to peter out at an old snow-pit, 50 metres below the antennae. 5 metres above the pit, a tiny sheep path heads toward a solitary pine tree just below the *coll*. The path soon disappears, but maintaining direction (SE), we climb to the pine tree, from where it's an easy 30 metre scramble up to the *coll* (Wp.10 180M) and over the low fence onto the ridge.

Some walkers turn left here, directly onto the first part of the ridge. This is both undesirable and indescribable. The rocks are so steep, the fissures so deep, the *carritx* covered boulders so treacherous, it's like dancing on needles, and a few hundred metres can mean forty minutes of blood, sweat and tears (not necessarily in that order). From the *coll*, descend directly to the dirt track 50 metres below the southern side of the ridge. This seems crazy after all the climbing, but I assure you, it's not. The track is fenced off, but never mind -

just get over, under or through that fence, as if your life depended on it (it doesn't quite, but after ten minutes dancing on the needles, you may well believe it does). We made the mistake of trying the full ridge route before giving it up as a bad job (sweat and tears, no blood) and descending to the dirt track, so the timing between Wps.10 & 11 is estimated.

Once past the fence, turn left. After about 500 metres, the dirt track dips down then climbs steeply toward the westernmost rocks (clearly visible) flanking the **Alfábia** peak. Going through a gap in the fence (Wp.11 195M), we pass a broad platform and catch sight again of the **Jovenolles** refuge below us, after which the track dwindles to a stony path crossing a rockspill to climb behind the first outcrop of rocks on the main ridge. The 'path' is really just a succession of ways, climbing steeply and winding through the *carritx*, but staying just behind the ridge and maintaining a generally easterly direction, we eventually see to our left the tall white trig point of the **Alfábia** summit (Wp.12 215M), an easy 20 metre scramble for a birds-eye view of the **Sóller** plain, the **Orient** valley, and the entire **Tramuntana**.

Returning to the 'path' and bearing left (E), we pass that welcome harbinger of civilisation, a cairn! But don't get too excited. We're now entering virtually pathless terrain and the cairns are minimal. Passing between the summit and the next mini-ridge, we traverse the northern side of the ridge before climbing to a tiny pass beside a second small top (Wp.13 225M). We now skirt the southern side of the mini-ridge, staying on the rock, till the cairns take us across rough, virtually pathless terrain down to a broad *coll*, from where we can see **Orient** village and the white sanctuary within **Castell d'Alaró**.

Still following the cairns, we climb a slight rise for our first sight of the **Cúber Reservoir**. Fifty metres beyond the rise, we cross a wall beside a large cairn at what appears to be its northern tip (Wp.14 240M). In fact, the wall continues on the far side. Bearing left, we follow the cairns on a route parallel to the wall, descending into a shallow depression dotted with oak. The occasional cairns are hidden in the trees here and are harder to spot, but maintaining direction (NE) and running parallel to the wall till it ends, we eventually climb out of the wooded depression toward a large cairn.

Cairns are scarce here, but continuing on rough limestone debris, we aim between **Puig Major** and a distinct upright stone marking a small top slightly to the left. The debris gives way to ridges and slanting sheets of rock as we skirt the head of a shallow gully on our left, after which we can climb to the upright stone (Wp.15 255M) where we get our first glimpse (to the right, in line with **Puig Major**) of the **Es Cornadors** refuge.

Returning to the shallow depression behind the upright stone and keeping the next small peak ('Small Peak X') to our left (take care, there is at least one deep pothole here), we see the **Cúber Reservoir** more clearly again, and pick our way with infinite patience across the increasingly fractured and treacherous rockscape, <u>heading all the time for **Puig Major**</u> (no cairns here). 200 metres after **Small Peak X**, we come to another wall, which we cross beside a rusted black and white private hunting sign (Wp.16 270M).

The reservoir disappears from sight again and we continue our painstaking progress across the limestone and *carritx*, staying about 30 metres behind the cliffs, still heading for **Puig Major**, and passing the very occasional cairn -

well, one actually!

Alfábia cliffs from Sementer Gran

We now have to pass to the <u>left</u> of **Sementer Gran**, the last summit on the ridge. **Cúber** comes back into view as well as the dirt track descending to the **Ofre** farm, at which point we start bearing left towards **Sementer Gran**, just before which we can see **Ofre** farm itself.

Skirting to the left of the peak with impressive views of the cliffs behind us, we come back into sight of the **Es Cornadors** refuge (currently being restored), where we can see that ineffable luxury, a real path!

First though we have to follow the rough cairn marked way down to the junction of paths (left up to the refuge and the *mirador*, right down to **Sóller**) at the *coll* 50 metres below the refuge, where there is a concrete marker post (Wp.17 295M). Given that we've probably had more than enough views and climbs for the day, we turn right for **Sóller**.

We now really stretch our legs out on the well-made path zigzagging down to the **Barranc de Biniaraix**. Don't stretch your legs out too far, though - the gravel is loose and accidents tend to happen in the stupidest places. Ignore all branch paths and stick to the main path, finally fording (the bridge has been swept away) the torrent (Wp.18 320M) just below Wp.5 of Walk 14, which we follow back to **Sóller** (405M).

Due to the military installations, **Puig Major**, Mallorca's highest mountain, is off limits. Fortunately, access to the **Bini Gran** farm at its base is unrestricted and we get a good feel for the area following the **Camí des Cingles** or 'Cliff Path'. Most of the walking is on dirt tracks and clear paths, but the stretch between Wps. 4&11 requires <u>excellent</u> pathfinding skills. However, if you're prepared to spend a bit of time scouting around for the 'path', it's hugely rewarding. The short versions and strolls avoid all pathfinding problems.

4*   3½-4H **   11.5 km   400m / 400m   ⟳   0

 *   Short Versions **(a)** & **(b)** 3 walker
** allow extra time for pathfinding
     Short Versions **(a)** 2 h (estimated) **(b)** 3 h one-way (estimated)

Short Versions	**Strolls**
(a) bear right at Wp.3 and descend as far as the concrete bridge **(b)** if you come by bus (which means walking from the C-710 to Wp.1), continue on the dirt track after the **Coll des Cards Colers** to catch the return bus from km38 of the C-710.	Anywhere up to Wp.3. Obvious turning points are the natural *mirador* after Wp.2, the stand of oak 200 metres after the **Bini Gran** gate, and **Font Subauma**.

Access: by car and bus (seasonal timetable).

Immediately behind the parking area on the sharp bend at km 2.2 of the PM-214-1 (Wp.1 0M), old red arrows indicate the start of our stony path (<u>not</u> the broader trail bearing right) climbing steadily (SW) towards the metal electricity pylons. Passing under the electricity cables, we bear right (W) to go through a gap in a stone wall next to a roofless ruin (Wp.2 15M). 200 metres after the wall, we pass a small and possibly dry spring, then go through a metal gate marked 'Bini Gran' (25M).

Climbing steadily after Wp.1

Descending along a partially cobbled trail, we pass a stand of oak and cross a watercourse below the towering **Puig Major** cliffs. Ignoring minor branches onto the surrounding terraces, we stick to the main path which gradually widens to a trail as it approaches a small cave extended by a tin roof, just below which is **Font Sabauma**. 30 metres after the *font*, we go through a large green metal gate (Wp.3 40M), where our trail becomes a track running into the main **Bini Gran** access track.

For **Short Version (a)** bear right. For the full version and **Short Version (b)** bear left.

The track climbs steadily, soon bringing us into view of fields and farmhouses below and, at the head of the **Bini Valley**, the woods and cliffs we must negotiate on our way down. It's worth pausing here to fix these in our mind to help orient ourselves on our descent. The track climbs (on the whole gently but with one or two steeper stretches) to the **Coll de Cards Colers**, where we turn right toward a tall metal cross set in a concrete and breeze-block pillar with a stone altar in front of it (Wp.4 80M). Take care here as several cairn marked routes to the right of the cross end on precipitous clifftops!

Keeping the cross on our right and our backs to **Puig Major**, we go to the right of the low walls of a ruin (W) to join a narrow, grassy path that climbs a slight rise to the west of the cliffs behind the cross, bringing us into view of the **Bini Valley**. Descending to the left of a small fenced field, we find a cairn (Wp.5 85M) 40 metres north of the field, marking the start of the descent. 15 metres below the cairn (NE) we find a path descending into the pine at the head of the valley.

Puig Major

The path winds down into the wood (though it's a moot point how long this sickly assembly of trees is going to last) gradually bearing round onto the right flank of the valley, where it steadily zigzags down to a particularly tall cairn (Wp.6 105M). Following a series of smaller cairns, we cross a canalised affluent of the main torrent and emerge from the trees before crossing the main watercourse 50 metres later. On our right, the remains of an old wall and a rock inset with a metal pole mark the top of what must once have been a spectacular waterfall. Since we're not water and don't fall with such impunity, we bear left to cross a virtually pathless stretch of *carritx* towards an outcrop of rock with a tiny cairn at its tip (about 75 metres away). From this cairn (Wp.7 110M) we can see the farm again. Passing the odd red waymark, we follow a broad rocky ledge behind the outcrop of rock before crossing a locked metal gate with a ladder stile.

Beyond the gate, a rough path leads into a second, healthier pine wood, which is where the real pathfinding problems begin. At first, all goes well. The path is badly overgrown with *carritx*, but is occasionally cobbled and dotted with red waymarks as it winds down the valley (ENE). But the *carritx* gradually gets denser and the winding turns to squirming as the 'path' descends towards the bed of the watercourse, which may be audible in spring. Beware! Despite a puzzling line of cairns that descend all the way down to a fence along the watercourse, we have to bear left (E) about 50 metres above the watercourse (Wp.8 120M) to pass under two fallen pines, shortly after which there is a distinct halved-circle waymark - needle in haystack, I know, but we found it!

Thirty metres after the waymark, we bear left on a very rough path climbing past a cairn to a mini-*coll* (Wp.9 125M) crossing a small, sharp ridge of rock, from where we can again see the farmhouses. Twenty metres below the *coll*, a clear path descends through another gate (probably open). It's worth turning back at the gate to see the remarkable eye drilled through the rock by erosion. After about 75 metres following the contour lines (NW), the path seems to

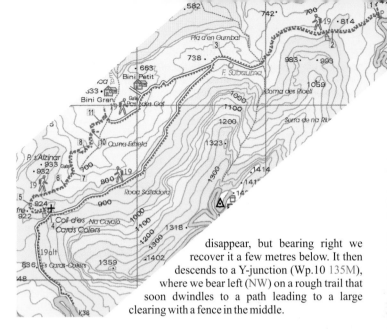

disappear, but bearing right we recover it a few metres below. It then descends to a Y-junction (Wp.10 135M), where we bear left (NW) on a rough trail that soon dwindles to a path leading to a large clearing with a fence in the middle.

Turning right just before the clearing, we follow a broad track through the woods, passing a corrugated tin shelter and crossing a green stile to the left of a large metal gate (Wp.11 140M). We then join another track and clamber over a locked green gate (no stile but an easy climb) onto a concrete bridge over the torrent. Ignoring the *Prohibido el Paso* sign and a branch track to the right, we follow the main track, bearing left at a Y-junction 100 metres later. The track skirts the farm, climbing gently to pass through another green gate (probably open) where we join the main access track for a steady climb back to our outward route, 100 metres from Wp. 3 (165M), forty minutes from the start.

This tiny but testing little walk is ideal at the end of the day or for motorists who've descended the tortuous **Sa Calobra** road (an extraordinary trip in itself), but don't have much time. The walk itself is unremarkable, but the **Mola de Tuent** *torre*, chapel and customs hut, are exceptional, beautifully restored and with superb views in all directions.

Access: by car – or on foot if staying in **Sa Calobra** or **Cala Tuent**.

We start from the car-park beside **Sant Llorenç** 'church' (a chapel in all but name) on the *coll* above **Cala Tuent** (Wp.1 0M). Behind the house attached to the chapel we take a gravelly path, climbing steeply to the small cliffs north of the *coll*. Shortly before the wall at the top of these cliffs, we pass a vertiginous stretch where a steel cable has been set in the rock (well-set at the time of writing, but test it before trusting your weight to it). N.B. If you find this passage at the limit of the tolerable on the way up, don't insist and simply turn back, as it's more alarming in descent. If you do insist and find yourselves in difficulty on the way back, descend with your back to the drop, which is a lot less hypnotic when you're not looking at it!

Beyond the wall above this cable we come onto a cistus-covered slope from where we already have fine views back towards **Puig Mayor**. Winding through dense cistus interspersed with the odd clump of *carritx* and *pistacia*, we climb steadily (NNE) on a faint, occasionally slightly confusing path. The path seems to end in a patch of barer ground just below the second outcrop of rocks (Wp.2 20M), but orienting ourselves by a small retaining wall, we maintain our general direction (N) winding through the cistus. Bearing left (SW) at a second cairn then right (NW) 50 metres later, we climb through waist high cistus, thyme, *carritx* and *pistacia* before emerging within sight of the **La Mola** buildings (Wp.3 25M). The path remains crazily overgrown and from a distance is invisible, but heading for the *torre*, the way clarifies itself as we progress. Passing just left of twin pines and ignoring the apparently clearer way through the *carritx* patch on our left, we continue wading through cistus (now chest deep), finally climbing up between the chapel and customs hut, thirty metres west of the tower (Wp.4 35M).

La Mola

The views are stunning, but even more stunning is the quality of the restoration work in this inaccessible site. The buildings are locked, but benches and a few grassy patches in the shade of trees make ideal picnic spots. Return by the same route.

Easy walking along a lovely corniche path to the superbly situated house at **Sa Costera**, with an optional excursion to the **Fábrica de Luz** hydro-electric generating station. Traditionally part of the **Ses Barques/Sa Calobra** route, returning by boat.

* + 35M for the extension and at least an hour for exploring and picnicking
** + 150 metres for the extension
*** in **Cala Tuent**

Short Version	**Stroll**	**Extension**
To La Fábrica and back (see text)	(a) bear right at Wp. 2 on the **Tuent/Es Vergeret** path back to the restaurant. (b) to the **Coll de ne Pollo**.	**La Fábrica** (see text).

Access: by car or boat.

We start from the **Cala Tuent Bar/Restaurante** on a dirt track between **C'an Boy** and the restaurant gates, signposted 'Sa Costera, Fornalutx, Sóller' (Wp.1 0M). After 100 metres, we pass a branch track and turn right on a signposted partially cobbled path. Climbing through the woods, we come to a third signpost (Wp.2 7M) below a broad dirt track, which we follow till it ends 75 metres later.

Cala Tuent

Recovering the cobbled trail, we climb to another dirt track in front of a large, tastefully restored farmhouse, where we turn right. When the track bears left 50 metres later, we take the waypoint path on the right (Wp.3 12M). After a short level stretch, the path climbs gently through mixed woodland, crossing a glade glazed with pine needles and going through a gap in a wall onto the **Coll de ne Pollo**, where views along the coast open out. **Sa Costera** is the house below the wood on the distant headland.

The path descends below a high, dry water chute before climbing to pass the first of two gateways with stone hinge brackets. After the second gateway, a clear green field and large reservoir behind **La Fábrica** are visible down to our right. Shortly after a bizarre rock formation that looks like a huge teetering cairn, we come to the signposted path down to 'La Fábrica/Font des Verger' (Wp.4 50M).

Extension / Short Version
Descending 150 metres only to climb right back up again is never a very engaging proposition, but I strongly recommend this extension. Taking the green-arrowed path to the right, we descend steeply, soon coming into view of

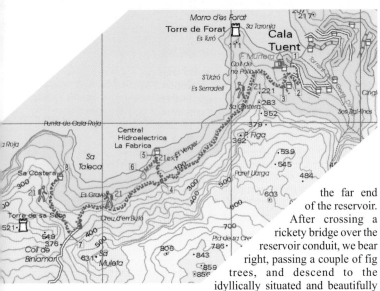

the far end of the reservoir. After crossing a rickety bridge over the reservoir conduit, we bear right, passing a couple of fig trees, and descend to the idyllically situated and beautifully restored generating station (Wp.5 15M from Wp.4). If you want to swim, the steps down to the turbines in front of the main buildings also lead to a tunnel onto what was once a jetty, just to the right of which a rope helps us descend onto the rocks. Turning left at the rickety bridge leads to the spring feeding the conduit (Wp.6). We return by the same route (20M).

To continue to Sa Costera
We follow the main path (W) along long level stretches interrupted by brief and sometimes not so brief climbs. After a clearing on our right, the path widens to a track and we continue climbing for a little over five minutes before taking a wayposted shortcut to the right (Wp.7 80M [not counting the extension]). Thirty metres later, we turn right at another waypost and leave the main trail. Descending along a *carritx* lined path, we bear left at a Y-junction and go through a gap in a wall, after which we follow a terrace to **Sa Costera** (Wp.8 100M), notable for a solar panel supplying a bell that chimes the hours, a mariner's toilet lovingly restored by 'Marti', and (50 metres NW) a tunnel housing a spring. Our return by the same route takes one hour and twenty minutes.

The **Torrent de Pareis**, Europe's second largest gorge, is Mallorca's most challenging and popular adventure excursion. However, it can't really be called a 'walk' as some climbing is involved and previous publications have received complaints that it was inappropriate in a walking guide. Bearing this in mind, we developed The Old English Sheepdog Trial, reasoning that anywhere we could go with an Old English Sheepdog, others could follow unencumbered. If you do intend doing the entire descent, enquire first about conditions at the **Serra Tramuntana Information Centre**. Though not essential, a short rope (5-6 metres) is useful for the full descent. Under no circumstances venture into the gorge if there's a risk of rain or the rocks are wet – unless you're one of the daredevils who descend during the winter when it's in full flood; but if you were, you wouldn't be reading a book like this.

(a) BOTTOM UP

This, the easiest of the three routes, is also perhaps the most spectacular, taking us to the mouth of the narrowest part of the gorge. It's not a stroll though and good boots are essential. Take care on the smoother rocks where there's only one way through: so many people have passed, the rocks are not so much polished as burnished. If you want to avoid the crowds (and I mean crowds; just look at the coach-park), arrive early. **Sa Calobra** itself is a splendid little site. What has been done with is somewhat less splendid, but at least it's still public and not smothered in concrete.

*in **Sa Calobra**

Access: on foot from **Sa Calobra** (accessible by car, boat and bus)

Descending from the **Sa Calobra** car-park, we bear right onto the promenade (0M), at the end of which we go through two dimly lit tunnels onto the pebbly beach at the bottom of the torrent, where we bear right, heading toward the interleaved walls of the gorge. The gorge gradually narrows and, next to an emergency-services sign, we come to a permanent pool (20M). To the left of the pool, we clamber through a natural tunnel formed by an immense rock and the canopy of a fig tree, after which the rocks get bigger, the walls get taller, and we get smaller. Passing a second large fig tree, we cross a slab of rock, after which we start boulder-hopping and squeezing between massive sculpted rocks (there's definitely a touch of the Henry Moores about some of them).

At an immense rock (30M) almost completely blocking the way, the trail appears to bear left, though this in fact ends at a large pool. We bear right to scramble over the rocks. 75 metres later, we bear right again, passing under a looming cavern onto a 50 metre flat stretch leading to the next jumble of boulders (38M). Following the clearly burnished trail, we climb across the middle of the rocks, and approach the narrowest section of the gorge, marked by a distinct menhir-like rock (43M). The gorge narrows even more, the cliffs climb higher, we continue shrinking. Passing a dripping mossy rock with a small fig tree sprouting from its centre, we squeeze to the left of a long low rock virtually blocking the gorge.

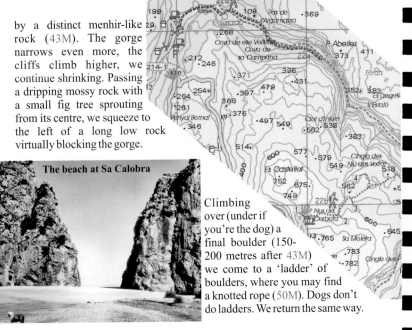

Climbing over (under if you're the dog) a final boulder (150-200 metres after 43M) we come to a 'ladder' of boulders, where you may find a knotted rope (50M). Dogs don't do ladders. We return the same way.

The beach at Sa Calobra

(b) SIDE ON

Hundreds of people stop at the **Nus de Corbata** (Tie Knot) **Mirador** everyday, but none of them seem to realise the car-park is no *mirador* at all. The real *mirador*, to my mind at least, is about a kilometre away at the end of a pathless descent through dense *carritx* and confusing masses of limestone. It's called the **Cingle des Niu des Voltor**, **Vulture's Nest Cliff**, a name that says it all really. Though the walk is short, this is just about the most isolated, little visited spot described in the entire book – take a friend! Also, good boots, long trousers and plenty of water. Rough walking, only for experienced walkers. Beware of rocks hidden by the *carritx*, a perfect man-trap ideal for twisting ankles.

*the Mirador bar is not recommended

Access: by car or bus

From the far end of the **Nus de Corbata** car-park (Wp.1 0M) we follow a faint track that descends towards **Puig Tomir** for 50 metres before petering out above a sheet of dumped bitumen. Ignoring cairns to the left (the start of one Very Mad Mallorcan loop round the **Clot d'Infern**), we maintain direction (ENE) picking our way over the *carritx* and crossing a rocky shelf to find the first of a series of cairns guiding us through our pathless descent.

After crossing a succession of rock sheets, we bear slightly right (ESE) descending into dense vegetation above a gully. Carefully following the cairns (spaced every 5 metres or so), we wind up and down along the southern flank of the gully to an affluent (Wp.2 15M), where we bear left, descending initially in the bed of the affluent, then along its left bank. Towards the bottom, we re-cross the affluent and descend into the main gully where the walking is slightly easier and the cairns correspondingly fewer.

When the main gully swings left we bear right, passing an outcrop of rock at the head of a long shallow valley (Wp.3 30M). Ignoring cairns that seem to indicate a way along the southern flank of this valley, we descend directly into the valley (NE), aiming for the long roofless building visible on the far side of the gorge (the **Quartel des Carabiners** barracks). For purposes of orientation, the large rocky outcrop just in front of this ruin is the **Serra de ses Farines**. From our perspective, Wp.4 is to the left of this outcrop, Wp.5 to the right. At the bottom of the valley, we descend into a shallow depression, just before which you may see an ancient red waymark.

Winding through head high clumps of *carritx*, we cross the depression, on the far side of which we have a choice. Timings assume taking both options.

For a glimpse of the lower stretch of the Pareis and a panorama of uninterrupted rock and sea

We bear left (NNE) and walk alongside the ridge of rock on our left to a pass (Wp.4 55M) at the top of a long slope down to the cliffs. The view is slightly better if you scramble round onto the rocks on your right. Except for the protests of the odd eagle, the silence is absolute. Return to the shallow depression by the same route.

For a more spectacular view from the Vulture's Nest Cliffs

We follow the cairn-marked route (ENE), crossing the lip of the depression and aiming for a distinct eye drilled in the rock, just to the right of which there's a small plateau with a large shady rock (Wp.5 85M) and stunning views towards the **Entreforc** (the junction of the **Gorg Blau** and **Lluc** torrents). Take great care here – there is <u>no</u> long slope between you and the cliffs. Return to the **Nus de Corbata** by the same route.

(c) TOP DOWN

A 'peck' is perhaps being a trifle disingenuous for this arduous hike down to the head of the gorge, which is more of a mouthful really. Not recommended on a hot day, but an interesting approach during winter - subject to the usual safety precautions. You might be tempted once at the bottom to continue all the way to **Sa Calobra** rather than slog back up to the top. This temptation should be resisted as the descent between the **Entreforc** and the sea includes all the most difficult passages. If you want to do the full descent, come prepared. Do not improvise. Though laughably easy and little used, the stroll leads to one of the best viewing points overlooking the gorge.

*I haven't used the services, but the **Escorca Restaurant** has a fine terrace and an interesting dining room built into the rock.

Short Version	Stroll
150 metres after Wp.3, as the main path bears sharp left, continue NE toward the olive trees, for a pleasant picnic spot on a grassy *sitja* with great views.	For superb views, carry straight on for 75 metres at Wp.2 onto the long sloping shelf of rock. Note the spectacular rock arch on your left.

Access: by car and bus. Park on the rough ground just west of the **Escorca Restaurant** (km 25 C-710) rather than in the restaurant car-park.

We start at the western end of the restaurant car-park on a stony path descending between the crash barrier and a multilingual warning notice (Wp.1 0M). Going through a gate almost immediately, we follow a pleasant, shady path alongside terraced pasture, turning left after a second gate before bearing away from the fields (NW). At a metre high cairn (Wp.2 10M), we swing sharp left, following large cairns across the rocks to join a rocky path zigzagging downhill, the **Voltes Llargues** or **Long Bends**, rapidly bringing the gorge into view. Shortly after, we see the **Quartel des Carabiners** barracks and, nestling below **Puig Roig**, the **Coscona** cave houses, the path becomes a little unclear amid the *carritx*, but maintaining our general direction (NNW) we descend toward the top of low cliffs before veering towards the barracks (N) and winding down between rocks beside the partially charred trunk of a fallen tree (Wp.3 25M). We now head in a north-easterly direction before swinging back sharp left to resume our zigzagging descent.

Passing several confused stretches covered in *carritx*, we look out for cairns marking the easier way, sometimes on long zigzags, sometimes on steeper shortcuts (notably at Wp.4 35M). A long north-easterly zig toward the right of **Puig Roig**, during which the entrance to the gorge disappears from view, is followed by an equally long south-westerly zag, before we double back and take a second clear shortcut (Wp.5 40M), soon after which a left hand bend on a broad ledge brings us into view of the remaining, apparently clear zigzags down to the bottom. There is however one tricky spot: after passing under a fig tree, we reach large overhanging rocks. Ignoring the clear way climbing straight ahead, we take a narrow path on the right, descending steeply to the **Torrent de Lluc** (65M) just in front of the **Torrent des Boverons** water chute.

Bearing left, we follow the torrent, picking our way across massive boulders to a faint way through the trees below a cliff (on the left) with an indented watershed. About 50 metres before the gorge narrows, we should, in strict accordance with the Old English Sheepdog Trial, turn back. However, this would be a bit frustrating for bipeds, so I suggest you continue for a further five minutes, descending the easy rocks below the cliff and following the **Torrent de Lluc** to the junction with the **Torrent des Gorg Blau**, the **Entreforc** (90M), where the **Torrent de Pareis** (literally 'Twin Stream') officially begins. From here we may also venture up the **Gorg Blau** torrent to the entrance (no further) of **Sa Fosca**, a complex system of caves and subterranean lakes that can only be explored by fully-equipped, experienced potholers. We return by the same route.

The **Alquería** is the westernmost of the three peaks on our left as we approach the **Sóller** tunnel from **Palma**. It's not a route often walked by tourists, but it is popular with locals and justifiably so. The views are excellent, the middle stretch is pleasantly isolated, and it is nearly all easy walking on dirt tracks that are, for the most part, closed to traffic. There are excellent picnic spots on the peak and after Wp.7.

*40 min from **Bunyola**

Short Versions
(a) A thirty minute climb up the **Alquería** track offers fine views of **Bunyola**, the plain and the **Alquería**'s sister peaks, **Son Poc** and **Son Nassi**. **(b)** In reverse to Wp. 7 (ignore the 'Camino Cortado/Prohibido el paso' signs); easy walking to lovely picnic spots. Wp.9 is the first branch on the left along the **Biniforani Vell** lane.

Extension
If arriving by public transport or staying locally, start from **Bunyola** (see text)

Stroll
Same as extension

Access: by car, bus, train, and on foot from **Bunyola**

Extension

From **Bunyola** church (Wp.1 0M) take the **Carrer de Sant Mateu** (signposted 'Palma') and turn right opposite the **Costa de s'Estacio** street sign. After descending to the main car-park, take the narrow lane past the large ochre-coloured house, **Can Manuel**, for an attractive stroll between gardens and fields to the main road just south of the **S'Alquería d'Avall** farm driveway (Wp.2 20M): km 15.8 of the C-711, the starting point for motorists.

N.B. Previous reports suggest you cannot park here. In fact, there is room for a few cars and parking seems to be tolerated so long as it doesn't impede access to the driveway.

Taking the **S'Alquería d'Avall** driveway, we bear left just before the house and go through a gate to join a dirt track, which we follow for most of the ascent. Ignoring all branch tracks and paths, we climb steadily through immaculately maintained olive terraces, passing a series of gates. The olives gradually give way to holm-oak, which are in turn interspersed with pine as the views open out across the plain and towards **Bunyola**. Eventually, just after a twin sheepfold, we come to a *coll* where a post topped with a cairn indicates a rough path on the left up to the **Mirador Leandro Ximenis** (Wp.3 80M). Leaving the track, we follow this path past a metal stile and three-sided shelter to the peak (Wp.4 90M), where we have superb views through 360°.

Returning to the dirt track, we bear left for a pleasant stroll passing two gates. After the second gate and directly behind a three-sided hut housing an old cart, we leave the main track and turn right on a minor track (Wp.5 105M) through an olive grove. After 100 metres the track swings left to cross the olive grove, but we maintain direction (N) for another 100 metres to the end of the olive grove, where an oak forested slope drops steeply away into the **Biniforani** valley. Bearing slightly left, we find a small cairn marking the head of a remarkable little defile, the **Pas de Sa Fesa** (Wp.6 110M).

Pas de Sa Fesa

We descend through the pass, crossing a high-stiled gate midway, to join a steep dirt path zigzagging down through the holm-oak. Towards the bottom, we pass a well-preserved *sitja* and bear left on a gentler slope marked by cairns. We then double back to a large pillar with an iron hinge bracket and descend onto a narrow track above abandoned olive terraces (Wp.7 125M).

Turning left, we wind down through the terraces, crossing a low fence next to green metal gates, after which we join a partially concreted track (Wp.8 135M) leading to a new house. Bearing right, we follow this track through a second set of green gates and, ignoring branches to right and left, continue our descent into the valley, passing a tennis court and a large sunken lemon grove, where we join the tarmac lane (Wp.9 150M) to the **Biniforani Vell** farmhouse. Turning right, we follow this lane for fifteen minutes down to the road, 40 metres north of Wp.2

An attractive tour along mostly shady paths and tracks through the lovely, well-managed forest of **Bunyola**. If you're after solitude, best avoided on a Sunday. If, on the other hand, you care to witness the glorious spectacle of Spanish families enjoying themselves at their gregarious best (just count the generations), Sunday at the **Cas Garriguer Área Recreativa** is a must. To drive or cycle to **Cas Garriguer**, turn left off the PM-202 just before the playground and follow **Carrer del Garrigó**, signposted 'Sa Comuna'.

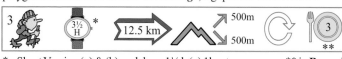

*   Short Version (a) & (b) each loop 1½ h (c) 1h return   . ** in **Bunyola**

Short Versions	Strolls
(a) turn right after Wp.4 to descend via **Comellar d'en Cupí** **(b)** drive to **Cas Garriguer Área Recreativa** then walk back to Wp.6 to join the main walk **(c)** as per Stroll 'c' but continue to **Cas Garriguer**	**(a)** from Wp.2 continue down the lane back into **Bunyola** **(b)** in almost any direction from the **Área Recreativa** **(c)** drive along the PM-202 past the cemetery. Turn left at the electricity substation, signposted 'Es Cocons', then carry straight on when the main lane bears left (Wp.10). Park on the flat open area (probably with a pile of rubbish in the middle) after **Can Co** and walk up to the troglodytic dwelling.

Access: on foot from **Bunyola**.

From **Bunyola** church (Wp.1 0M), we take **Carrer Mare de Deú de la Neu** past the post office to cross **Calle de Santa Catalina Tomás** and climb the stairway street, **Carrer de la Lluna**. Turning right at the top, we follow **Carrer d'Orient**, ignoring a first stairway to a private house before turning left onto another stairway street, **Carreró de la Comuna**, signposted 'Sa Comuna/Camí des Grau'. Circling the **Villa Teresa**, we climb to a dirt lane leading towards the mottled bluffs of **El Castellet**. When the lane dips down after 100 metres, we turn left on the **Camí d'es Grau** (Wp.2 10M).

Our path climbs steadily (NE) through the woods to the left of the bluffs, passing the first of the red dots that partially waymark our route. Ignoring all branches, we pass a restored lime-kiln, *sitja* and *aljub* before reaching a Y-junction (Wp.3 25M) where we bear right. After levelling off briefly the **Camí des Grau** continues climbing, zigzagging up to a less well defined stretch winding through the pine. A pleasant meander through the woods brings us to a junction with a broader trail signposted 'Mirador/Camí des Grau' (Wp.4 40M). *Mirador* is a big word for a small clearing on the cliffs with a fallen tree for a bench, but it's only 40 metres to our left, and the views are good.

Continuing on the broad trail, we cross a slight rise before joining a dirt track (signed 'Bunyola/Comellar d'en Cupí'), on which we continue climbing through a shallow gully shrouded by a canopy of trees to a major junction of dirt tracks (Wp.5 55M).

Turning right, we pass a green fire-fighting reservoir, 50 metres after which we join the main track to **Cas Garriguer** (Wp.6 60M). Ignoring the main track, we immediately bear left on a broad, gated branch track.

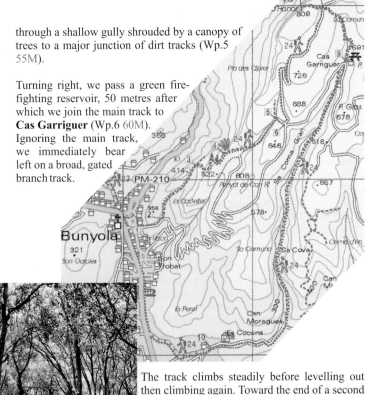

Bunyola woods

The track climbs steadily before levelling out then climbing again. Toward the end of a second long, level stretch, we turn left onto a clear path marked by a cairn and signpost (Wp.7 85M). A steady climb of a little under ten minutes brings us to the white rock of the *penyal*, where there's a small green hut that looks alarmingly like an ice-cream kiosk, but is presumably a weather station (Wp.8 95M). After enjoying the spectacular view, we retrace our steps to Wp.7.

Opposite the path to the *penyal*, another path, almost invisible from the track but marked by a small cairn, descends steadily then steeply before widening and levelling out for a gentle stroll to the last bend in the main track (Wp.9 115M) above the **Cas Garriguer Área Recreativa**. Descending to the turning circle in front of the forest warden's hut (there's also a public refuge - the key is available from **Bunyola** town hall), we maintain direction (SSW) on a broad trail passing picnic tables and barbecues. We follow this trail and the lane it leads into all the way back to **Bunyola**, passing through perhaps the most attractive woodland landscape on the entire island. You don't want to be reading a book while you're wandering through this exquisite wood, so in brief: after thirty minutes the track goes through a green wooden gate and continues between walled olive groves; five minutes later we pass a troglodytic house; just after the **Villa Maria**, we join a lane (Wp.10 180M); ten minutes on this lane brings us to the PM-202 behind the electricity substation, where we bear right for a fifteen minute walk along the road back to **Bunyola**.

Castell d'Alaró is a <u>very</u> popular walking destination and is best avoided at weekends. Even during the week it's as well to leave early to get there before the guided hiking parties. Most people climb from **Alaró**, but if you have a car, the **Orient** route, on a pleasant, frequently shady path, is far more attractive. Even taking the waymarked shortcuts, the southern approach involves a good three kilometres of wearying tarmac and concrete. The only advantage, apart from public transport, is a more dramatic perspective on the cliffs that made the castle nigh on impregnable (it withstood a siege for two years). The extension, virtually pathless and almost indescribable, is only recommended for those navigating with a GPS 'GoTo' function or the fortunate few possessed of supernatural pathfinding skills.

* + 1h for the extension, Short Version 50M
** + 100 metres for the extension
*** The sanctuary can serve 40 and sleep 17, but book if you want to stay or, on weekends, even eat (Tel: 971 182112). The bar's open from 9am-11pm, the kitchen from 12am-4pm & 7-10pm.

	Short Version
Extension see text	Drive to Wp.2 and start from there. Turn west just south of km18 on the PM-210 then first right and follow the tarmac/concrete lane past **Es Verger Restaurant** (km 4.5) to **Es Pouet** (km 7) where it ends: note, after the restaurant the track gets even narrower!

Access: by car.

Just after km 11.8 of the PM-210, 150 metres east of the **Hermitage Hotel**, we take a track climbing into olive groves via a waymarked gate with two signs prohibiting dogs (Wp.1 0M). The broad, chalky white track climbs gently (NE) before narrowing to a well trodden path running along the edge of a terrace. The climb gradually steepens and the path bears right into a shady oak wood. The gradient eases slightly as the oak are interspersed with pine, before a final steady climb brings us onto a track (Wp.2 35M) at the bottom of the gently shelving clearing of **Es Pouet**.

At the top of the clearing, we bear left at the 'Alaró/Santuari y Postat Hostatgeria del Castell d'Alaró' signpost onto long, shallow steps leading to a partially cobbled trail. At the junction with the path from **Alaró** (Wp.3 50M), we bear left and follow the remaining steps up to the castle gates.

After exploring (cautiously!) the battlements along the west of the ridge, we follow the stone trail (E) up to the sanctuary (Wp.4 60M). Taking the partially ramped steps to the right of the chapel and climbing to the aerial, we can see (E) **Alaró**'s twin peak, **s'Alcaldena**.

Extension

The path to the **Cova de San Antoni** is so obscure it barely exists, but even those wholly lacking a sense of direction can enjoy wandering round the woods to the east, visiting the lime-kilns and *aljibes*. For the more adventurous, cairns mark the way down to the cave, which can be explored, but only with the utmost care and NOT when it's wet.

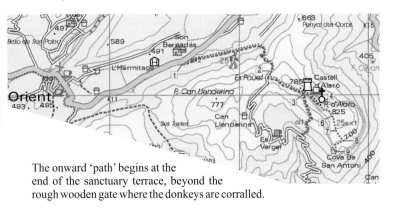

The onward 'path' begins at the end of the sanctuary terrace, beyond the rough wooden gate where the donkeys are corralled.

GPS users turn to their 'GoTo' function here, but be careful: there's no such thing as a straight line through these woods and you still need to follow the cairns carefully. After Wp.6, if you haven't seen a cairn in the preceding 30 metres, go back to the last cairn and look again. The route takes about twenty-five minutes each way. Given the inevitable pausing, peering and backtracking required to find the cairns, partial times are redundant, but the following waypoints were taken at roughly five minute intervals.

At first the path is reasonably clear, passing an outdoor privy and winding between rocks (ESE) to cross two linked clearings (Wp.5). Continuing through the woods (SE), look for a third clearing (Wp.6) a few metres to the right of the main path, where we bear right to pass a lime-kiln. We now follow the cairns in a more southerly direction, passing Wp.7 (solely a GPS bearing, indistinguishable from the surrounding woodland) and steadily descending until, off to our right, we can see a partially ruined watchtower perched on the cliffs (Wp.8). Bearing right (SW), we follow a reasonably clear path down to the tower (Wp.9). The entrance to the cave is a small hole, 15 metres before the tower. We return via the same route. The descent from the sanctuary to the starting point takes about forty minutes.

This attractive circuit through the woods above **Orient** offers something for everyone. Picnickers can stroll along a drovers' track to a lovely shady stream, more energetic walkers can follow the Short Version for a fine woodland circuit, and the adventurous can do the full version with its exhausting scramble up the overgrown bed of the **Torrent d'es Bous**. The full version shouldn't be undertaken when it is wet, or in any circumstances by anyone who doesn't positively like plunging through pathless woodland with only the occasional cairn for guidance. The bushes aren't thorny, but long trousers are advisable between Wps.4 & 6. Don't attempt Wps.4-6 in reverse unless you happen to be two feet tall and have a stout visor. If you don't like road walking, park at Wp.1 and turn left at the junction just before Wp.7, skipping **Orient**.

* Short Version 2   ** Short Version 1h 20   (U)   *** in **Orient**

Short Version
Bear left at Wp.3 and climb directly to the pass (see text)

Stroll
To **Torrent d'es Freu**, Wp.2

Extension
Not mapped by us, but it should be possible to continue from Wp.4 all the way to **Santa Maria del Camy**, or bear right at Wp.6 and descend to **Alaró**. For the second option, it might be more logical to follow the Short Version and turn right just before Wp.7 at the rock pond.

Access: by car. Park in **Orient** or near Wp.1 (space looks limited at Wp.1, but on Sundays hundreds of locals contrive to cram their cars along the roadside, so you should be able to park somewhere!).

From **Orient**, we follow the PM-210 (W) for a little over 1.5 kilometres to km 9.6, where we turn left onto the 'Santa Maria' track (Wp.1 20M). Crossing a stile 75 metres later, we follow a stony trail flanked by dry stone walls.

Ignoring two branches to the right, we continue along the main trail, passing the high wall of a ruin and crossing a metal gate/stile (Wp.2 35M), beyond which stepping stones cross the **Torrent d'es Freu** to a second 'Santa Maria' signpost indicating our path to the left.

The stony drovers' trail

After a steady climb, the path veers left through a gap in a wall, immediately after which there's a faint crossroads and, one minute later, a wayposted junction with a broad walking trail (Wp.3 45M).

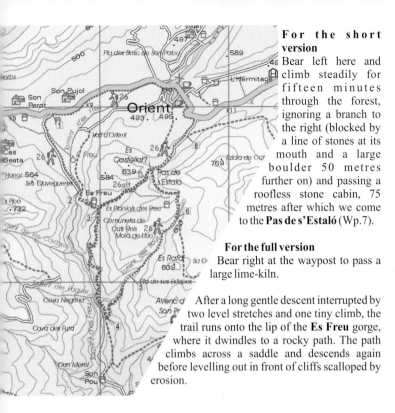

Bear left here and climb steadily for fifteen minutes through the forest, ignoring a branch to the right (blocked by a line of stones at its mouth and a large boulder 50 metres further on) and passing a roofless stone cabin, 75 metres after which we come to the **Pas de s'Estaló** (Wp.7).

For the full version

Bear right at the waypost to pass a large lime-kiln.

After a long gentle descent interrupted by two level stretches and one tiny climb, the trail runs onto the lip of the **Es Freu** gorge, where it dwindles to a rocky path. The path climbs across a saddle and descends again before levelling out in front of cliffs scalloped by erosion.

Climbing left onto another broad trail (Wp.4 65M), we turn sharp left, leaving the main trail to follow a narrow path along a retaining wall. Climbing gently and then steadily, we bear right alongside a dry affluent of the **Es Freu**, the **Torrent des Bous**. The route becomes increasingly overgrown, but is at first relatively clear, as we follow the retaining walls. From hereon in we just keep heading up the torrent as best we can, but for those who want confirmation this actually is the 'way' a few details…

After passing a small *sitja* and ruined shelter, we come to an exposed rock shelf where the path (by now declining into a 'way') seems to disappear. Maintaining direction (NW), we soon pick it up again, sticking to the remains of the retaining wall and the erosion gully running alongside it. Unfortunately, the wall and gully don't stick with us and we are soon obliged to pick our way through the *carritx*, looking for patches where it has been flattened by water and feet. The way takes us onto the torrent's right bank, after which we begin to glimpse daylight at the head of the torrent and climb onto a 50 metre broad rock funnel (Wp.5 85M).

It's tempting to think you're almost at the top here, but in fact the most arduous stretch is yet to come. We now push through dense under and overgrowth, looking for cairns, and winding in and out of the watercourse (notably to avoid slippery patches of damp rock). After climbing to the head of a second, much longer, rougher rock funnel, we come to a small dry waterfall where the rocks are too smooth for easy scrambling and we bear right before doubling back to the bed of the torrent. Two cairns lead us across a stretch of debris, after which we follow an affluent parallel to the main torrent. Just after the low walls of a ruined shelter, cairns lead us back into the main torrent beside another ruined shelter.

The way becomes clearer (which inevitably means more and larger cairns!) and we climb steadily towards the light, passing a third, more substantial shelter, 10 metres behind which there are the remains of a small oven. Following the torrent, we come to what appears to be the watershed where we climb to the right of a dry waterfall. In fact, after crossing a *sitja* further up, we come to a second watershed, after which the way levels out, passing two more *sitjas*, at the second of which we finally emerge on a clear path (Wp.6 115M).

Turning left, we follow the clear path through the woods, climbing gently to cross a broken wall, where we bear slightly right and descend along a stony path passing a tiny reservoir, a stone cabin and a *sitja*. Bearing right (NW), away from the *sitja*, we continue on the path as it contours round the slope, passing the occasional yellow waymark. When the path comes to a large natural pond in the rock (possibly dry, but the junction of paths is obvious), we bear right to pass through the natural rock gateway of **Pas de s'Estaló** (Wp.7 130M). From the pass, we follow the broad walking trail (NW) down to a dirt track (135M), which we descend until a slight rise brings us to a large oak in front of a wooden gate (Wp.8 140M), where the track starts to climb more steeply. Turning left through the gate onto a minor track, we descend through a cherry orchard to the PM-210, 200 metres from **Orient** (150M).

To be honest, **Puig Massanella** is not my personal high point of walking in Mallorca, but it is the highest point open to the public and as such an essential challenge for many people. The traditional route is via the **Comafreda** farm, which means paying €4 for the privilege (see Appendix D). This little-known variation joins the **Comafreda** route <u>after</u> the toll has been collected. However, we do pay in other ways, adding 200 metres to an already gruelling climb and following a pathless route along the **Torrent de sa Coveta Negra**, much of which is blocked by fallen trees. Do not underestimate this walk. It's tough and should not be undertaken when the weather's hot. Pathfinding is a real problem. If going alone, let someone know the route you're following. Take at least two litres of water per person.

* allow plenty of extra time for pathfinding (U)	**Short Version**
	Stay on the main track at Wp.2 to join the **Cami Vell** (Walk 29, Wp.9). Return to the **Sa Coveta Negra Área Recreativa** following the road from the **Son Canta** farmhouse.
Access: by car and bus (from **Caimari**)	

The gates at the start of the route

We start from the **Sa Coveta Negra Área Recreativa** at km10 of the PM-213. 100 metres <u>after</u> the km10 milepost, we go through unlocked green gates (Wp.1 0M) to take a dirt track. <u>N.B. NOT the superficially similar track just before the milepost.</u> Climbing steadily, we pass a huge rock with a plaque commemorating 'Isabel Morel Morro', then turn first left on a track marked with a blue arrow and the initials 'J.M.' (Wp.2 20M).

Though clear at first, this track is rapidly swamped in vegetation and soon dwindles to a barely perceptible charcoal-burners' trail, winding up through an S-bend, at the top of which cairns indicate where we branch off to the right (Wp.3 25M). We now climb steadily through the woods, taking great care to follow the cairns and red waymarks, as we are decidedly off-path. If you haven't seen a cairn after 20 metres or so, turn back.

After a couple of hundred metres, the way swings left to cross a *sitja*, climbing to more sparsely wooded slopes but staying in the shade of the oaks and maintaining a generally north-westerly direction. Red arrows and cairns lead us through trees, *carritx* and rocks, up to the first of the felled trees that are such a bane on this route. After a final scramble over huge boulders, we cross the remains of two short walls and descend very slightly to pick our way (NW) across a slope littered with trees, 200 metres after which we descend to the bed of the torrent at the **Pas de n'Arbona**, identifiable by a double-ringed *sitja* (Wp.4 65M).

This is where the real pathfinding problems begin. The onward route does occasionally follow old charcoal burners' paths and is marked with cairns and red waymarks, but there are so many broken trees littering the way, it's almost impossible to find a consistently clear route. What we must bear in mind is that we follow the course of the torrent insofar as the trees allow. Ignore cairns that seem to indicate ways up to the right.

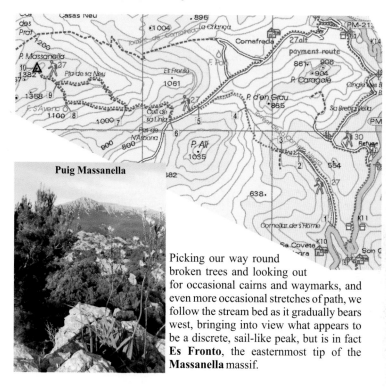

Puig Massanella

Picking our way round broken trees and looking out for occasional cairns and waymarks, and even more occasional stretches of path, we follow the stream bed as it gradually bears west, bringing into view what appears to be a discrete, sail-like peak, but is in fact **Es Fronto**, the easternmost tip of the **Massanella** massif.

Veering to the left of **Es Fronto**, we pass several *sitjes*, doubtless wishing they were still working and doing some damage to the innumerable dead trees impeding our progress: this is where you start to understand the origin of the phrase "we're not out of the woods yet". Finally, we come to a *sitja* with a clear track running in from the right, which leads up to the main **Comafreda** dirt track (Wp.5 90M). If you are not using the gps waypoints, it's worth marking this spot yourself in some way so you don't miss it on the way back.

Bearing left, we climb to the **Coll de sa Linia**, where two large gate-like stone marker posts indicate the onward track to 'Mancor', the way back to 'Lluc', and (sharp right) the path up to the *puig* (Wp.6 95M). Turning right between the posts, we take a good clear path marked with cairns and red waymarks winding up through the woods to a triangular concrete marker post (Wp.7 120M) indicating 'Font y Puig' on the left and 'Puig y Font' on the right.

The latter is the easier way to the top, but if you want to do the loop, I suggest passing by the **S'Avenc** spring first as a steep climb is less risky than a steep descent, especially on such viciously sharp limestone. Take care though – the spring route crosses rough, pathless terrain and there's a maze of divergent cairn-marked routes, most of which go nowhere! It's essential to follow the lower route marked with cairns AND red waymarks. If you find the cairns are getting increasingly infrequent and the waymarks have disappeared, you're on a false trail. Go back till you find regular cairns and waymarks. Particular care must be taken in the first 200 metres after the marker stone. ALWAYS look for the lowest cairns, even if the cairns climbing to the right seem to mark a clearer way.

Staying more or less on the level and only climbing very slightly (never steeply), we follow the cairns and waymarks (W) and, after about ten minutes, pass between two fallen trees and a large bushy oak, beyond which we start to climb, initially on rubble, but soon passing a sloping rock shelf with five marker steps cemented onto it. A steady climb across the rocks, passing waymarks, cairns and the occasional cemented marker-step, suddenly brings us abreast of the 'Font de s'Avenc' (Wp.8 130M) where steps descend to the spring and a damp shelter with rough stone benches and a table.

Just after the spring, cairns mark the way up the jagged limestone. A steep climb gradually brings us into view of the trig point on the peak. After passing another triangular marker stone (Wp.9 145M), the gradient eases briefly and, 100 metres later, we join the 'easy' path from the **Pla de sa Neu** or Snow Plain, where we bear left and begin our last long slog up to the top. Like many climbs, the last bit seems interminable, but it does eventually end (Wp.10 165M) with unrivalled views and horrible drops. Just below the summit, there's also an alarmingly deep pothole, once used as a snowpit.

The return takes about two hours. Picking our way back down to the junction of paths, we follow the well-marked 'easy' route across the **Pla de sa Neu** (E), until the path bears right (SSE) to a natural gateway leading onto a good, clear path zigzagging down to Wp.7. We then return via the same route, which is considerably easier to follow on the way down.

See the notes on GPS use and waypoints on pages 19-20.

9.
Port de Sóller - Sóller - Port de Sóller

Wp	N	E
1	39 47.7798	2 41.8044
2	39 47.6244	2 42.8856
3	39 47.0466	2 42.6570
4	39 46.3704	2 42.9612
5	39 47.3766	2 42.3888
6	39 47.8950	2 42.5814

10.
Three Villages + One Thundering Great Climb

Wp	N	E
1	39 46.2864	2 43.0344
2	39 46.6200	2 43.5648
3	39 47.0292	2 44.4282
4	39 47.5098	2 44.3844
5	39 47.5992	2 44.2326
6	39 47.4306	2 43.5030
7	39 47.1432	2 43.9302
8	39 46.9692	2 44.0694

11.
The Ultimate Picnic Walk - Torre Picada & Sa Illeta

Wp	N	E
1	39 47.8056	2 41.8002
2	39 48.1116	2 42.1242
3	39 48.3120	2 42.1272
4	39 48.3858	2 41.8362
5	39 48.5718	2 42.4824
6	39 48.8010	2 42.7818
7	39 49.1166	2 43.2984
8	39 48.9180	2 42.8022

12.
Capelleta & Campo

Wp	N	E
1	39 46.4172	2 43.2162
2	39 46.6962	2 43.3188
3	39 46.8450	2 43.3428
4	39 47.0676	2 43.3938
5	39 47.3580	2 43.2096
6	39 47.0628	2 42.9804

13.
Port de Sóller, the Mirador de ses Barques & the Balitx Valley

Wp	N	E
1	39 47.6226	2 42.8856
2	39 47.3592	2 43.2138
3	39 47.5518	2 43.4538
4	39 47.8026	2 43.5978
5	39 48.1884	2 43.6866
6	39 48.2556	2 43.8204
7	39 48.4056	2 43.9374
8	39 48.5808	2 44.3850
9	39 48.8088	2 44.4744
10	39 47.4552	2 43.4934
11	39 47.2542	2 43.4160
12	39 47.1456	2 43.4274

14.
Cúber Reservoir to Sóller

Wp	N	E
1	39 47.2386	2 47.8146
2	39 46.1622	2 46.0698
3	39 45.9630	2 45.7872
4	39 45.6432	2 45.5892
5	39 45.5976	2 45.3960
6	39 46.1982	2 44.0784

15.
Sa Rateta & L'Ofre from Cúber

Wp	N	E
1	39 47.2380	2 47.8140
2	39 46.8246	2 47.3790
3	39 46.6176	2 47.4726
4	39 46.5816	2 47.5032
5	39 46.4538	2 47.3040
6	39 46.4358	2 47.0694
7	39 46.2426	2 46.7220
8	39 46.1334	2 46.5570
9	39 45.9504	2 46.3554
10	39 45.8022	2 46.0194
11	39 46.2258	2 46.3818
12	39 46.2390	2 46.1508

16.
Tossals Verds Circuit

Wp	N	E
1	39 47.2272	2 47.9742
2	39 46.8486	2 47.5326
3	39 46.5246	2 48.1164
4	39 46.0170	2 48.6132
5	39 45.8688	2 48.8160
6	39 46.0992	2 49.1322
7	39 46.6182	2 49.8342
8	39 47.1678	2 49.8870
9	39 47.2716	2 49.7154
10	39 47.3118	2 49.5174
11	39 47.5242	2 49.4292

17.
Twin Peaks & One Mad

Mallorcan Loop

Wp	N	E
1	39 47.2458	2 47.9652
2	39 47.5284	2 49.4256
3	39 47.3136	2 49.5258
4	39 47.2494	2 49.3434
5	39 47.2086	2 49.1772
6	39 47.3598	2 49.1160
7	39 47.0046	2 49.0710
8	39 47.0526	2 49.2240
9	39 47.1516	2 48.8874
10	39 47.2248	2 48.6912
11	39 47.0850	2 48.4782
12	39 47.0394	2 48.3828
13	39 47.0382	2 48.3336
14	39 47.0286	2 48.1782
15	39 47.0610	2 48.0612

18.
The Alfábia Ridge

Wp	N	E
1	39 45.6942	2 43.1616
2	39 45.4770	2 43.1070
3	39 45.3774	2 43.1142
4	39 45.2250	2 42.9972
5	39 45.0894	2 42.9816
6	39 44.8674	2 42.9360
7	39 44.8212	2 42.9576
8	39 44.5710	2 42.9798
9	39 44.3940	2 43.0260
10	39 44.2398	2 43.2216
11	39 44.3976	2 43.6080
12	39 44.6016	2 43.9470
13	39 44.6562	2 44.1006
14	39 44.7870	2 44.3502
15	39 45.0096	2 44.4732
16	39 45.1272	2 44.6634
17	39 45.4944	2 44.8434
18	39 45.5550	2 45.3576

19
The Camí des Cingles below Puig Major

Wp	N	E
1	39 49.4928	2 48.8784
2	39 49.4232	2 48.5154
3	39 49.2792	2 47.6880
4	39 48.3942	2 46.3164
5	39 48.4398	2 46.1586
6	39 48.5346	2 46.4388
7	39 48.6420	2 46.4982
8	39 48.7404	2 46.5768
9	39 48.7782	2 46.6290
10	39 48.8448	2 46.6278

11 39 48.9120 2 46.7220

20.
La Mola de Tuent

Wp	N	E
1	39 50.5500	2 47.2248
2	39 50.7672	2 47.2254
3	39 50.7930	2 47.1660
4	39 50.8962	2 47.0160

21.
Cala Tuent - Sa Costera - Cala Tuent

Wp	N	E
1	39 50.3526	2 46.4940
2	39 50.2536	2 46.4742
3	39 50.2074	2 46.3854
4	39 49.6620	2 45.4578
5	39 49.7976	2 45.3906
6	39 49.7130	2 45.3228
7	39 49.3722	2 44.7528
8	39 49.6914	2 44.6502

22.
Three Pecks at the Torrent de Pareis

(b)

Wp	N	E
1	39 49.9230	2 48.9912
2	39 49.9446	2 49.2402
3	39 50.0370	2 49.3344
4	39 50.1900	2 49.4730
5	39 50.1840	2 49.6920

(c)

Wp	N	E
1	39 49.5726	2 50.8230
2	39 49.7778	2 50.6136
3	39 49.8750	2 50.4846
4	39 49.9434	2 50.5200

5 39 50.0184 2 50.4654

23.
Bunyola - Alquería - Bunyola

Wp	N	E
1	39 41.7636	2 41.9898
2	39 42.3696	2 41.3490
3	39 41.9808	2 40.4496
4	39 41.8374	2 40.4448
5	39 42.2358	2 40.3212
6	39 42.4482	2 40.3578
7	39 42.5688	2 40.4082
8	39 42.7260	2 40.4274
9	39 42.8958	2 40.7568

24.
Bunyola - Penyal d'Honor - Bunyola

Wp	N	E
1	39 41.7912	2 41.9700
2	39 41.7774	2 42.2958
3	39 42.0702	2 42.5316
4	39 42.1470	2 42.7626
5	39 42.3624	2 43.1874
6	39 42.3222	2 43.2420
7	39 42.9732	2 43.5276
8	39 42.9834	2 43.3686
9	39 42.6576	2 43.7064
10	39 41.0471	2 42.7222

25.
Castell d'Alaró & Cova de Sant Antoni

Wp	N	E
1	39 44.1948	2 46.5168
2	39 44.1300	2 47.2104
3	39 43.9620	2 47.5320
4	39 43.9500	2 47.5908
5	39 43.9104	2 47.6508
6	39 43.8816	2 47.7294
7	39 43.8060	2 47.7468
8	39 43.7478	2 47.7942
9	39 43.6740	2 47.7450

26.
Orient - Pas de s'Estalo - Orient

Wp	N	E
1	39 43.9302	2 44.5644
2	39 43.5150	2 44.8242
3	39 43.4202	2 44.9658
4	39 42.8040	2 45.0288
5	39 43.0434	2 45.2364
6	39 43.3626	2 45.5886
7	39 43.6410	2 45.4086
8	39 43.8360	2 45.6660

27.
Puig Massanella

Wp	N	E
1	39 47.4600	2 53.4540
2	39 47.8938	2 53.2224
3	39 47.8776	2 53.0934
4	39 48.1158	2 52.8276
5	39 48.1458	2 52.4514
6	39 48.0456	2 52.2624
7	39 48.1104	2 51.8850
8	39 48.1410	2 51.4284
9	39 48.2310	2 51.3546
10	39 48.3618	2 51.1788

EAST: LLUC TO THE COAST

A PLACE OF PILGRIMAGE, TORMENTED TREES AND TETHERED ISLANDS

The monastery at **Lluc** is in many ways the spiritual home of Mallorca. When the church was still the most potent trans-national institution in Europe, **Lluc** was the objective of traditional pilgrimages, many of which continue to this day, though socializing rather than salvation appears to be the prime motive now, even among avowedly Christian groups; with the advent of mass tourism, restaurants and an immense, charmless car-park were installed to accommodate package pilgrims for whom the church's function was principally decorative, more a focus for the camera lens. Nowadays the **Tramuntana Information Centre** at the monastery gates is a magnet for modern nature pilgrims, come to worship at the altar of landscape, flora and fauna, and practice their devotions on some of the island's finest footpaths.

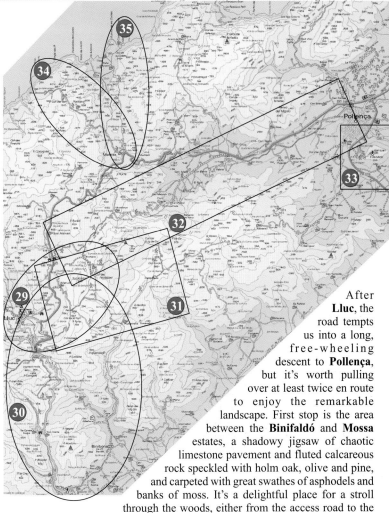

After **Lluc**, the road tempts us into a long, free-wheeling descent to **Pollença**, but it's worth pulling over at least twice en route to enjoy the remarkable landscape. First stop is the area between the **Binifaldó** and **Mossa** estates, a shadowy jigsaw of chaotic limestone pavement and fluted calcareous rock speckled with holm oak, olive and pine, and carpeted with great swathes of asphodels and banks of moss. It's a delightful place for a stroll through the woods, either from the access road to the **Binifaldó** bottling plant or one of the excellent *áreas recreativa* on the main road, which also happen to be among the few places on the island where camping is allowed.

Further down the C710, another tremendously privileged spot lies between the road and the northern coast, encompassed by the **Mortitx**, **Havanor** and **Rafal d'Ariant** estates. Everywhere you go in Mallorca, you'll be amazed by ancient olive trees twisted into incredibly contorted shapes, some so monolithic and gnarled by repeated pollarding, they resemble monstrous lumps of solid rock endeavouring, with invincible optimism, to pass themselves off as fruitful trees by the feeble ruse of decking themselves out with a few flimsy twigs and sprays of pale green leaves. George Sand compared these trees to fairytale monsters, while Rusiñol got so excited he

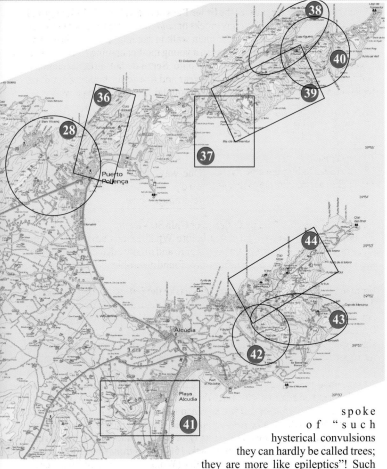

spoke
of "such
hysterical convulsions
they can hardly be called trees;
they are more like epileptics"! Such
images probably tell us more about the authors than the trees, but they serve to
convey a sense of the thousands of small, arboreal epiphanies to be
experienced on the island, and **Mortitx** is one the best places to enjoy them.

Eventually, the broad green valley behind **Pollença** opens out and we head
down to the eastern plain. The old towns of **Pollença** and **Alcúdia** are worth
visiting while their respective ports serve their purpose as tourist towns with a
full range of facilities, but the real stars at this end of the island are the two
peninsulas tipped by the **Caps de Formentor** and **Pinar**. The necks of these
peninsulas are in the first case so narrow and in the second so shallow they
look like they've been haphazardly moored to the main island and could as
easily be untethered and set adrift. This impression of being all at sea is
compounded as you drive onto **Formentor**, which appears to be composed of
a series of discrete sails, like a regatta of rock. Even if you haven't got a car,
hire a bike or taxi to get up to the **Coll de la Creuta** *mirador* for a glimpse of
this magnificent spectacle: you won't regret it.

This very popular walk crosses the **Siller Pass** between **Port de Pollença** and **Cala St. Vicenç** (actually four tiny creeks or *calas* clustered together in a large bay). It's very easy, you can do the main walk in sandals or tennis shoes, and ideal for a family stroll - I've even seen a young mother coming from **Cala St. Vicenç** with a pushchair! The extension onto **Serra de la Punta**, by contrast, is rough walking, requiring good footwear and a taste for hopping about on rocky terrain with nothing but cairns and mountain goats for company.

*	Extension 4
**	3h15 including the extension
***	+ 225 metres for the extension

Short Version	**Extension**
One-way from either end, arriving or returning by boat.	**Serra de la Punta**, see text.

Access: on foot from **Port de Pollença** or **Cala St. Vicenç**.
Update: report of locked gates just before Wp.2. Locals advise bypassing these by climbing a couple of low walls onto and off the adjacent land though this is not strictly legal; other walkers have found no problems (Oct 2005)..

From the seafront in **Port de Pollença**, we take the **Pollença** road (**Carrer de Joan XXIII**) and turn right at **Bar Juanito**, 20 metres before the ELF/Cepsa petrol station, on **Carrer de Cala St. Vicenç** (Wp.1 0M). Crossing the new bypass, we take **Carrer de les Roses** to the left of the beige house with blue shutters. Ignoring four branches on the right, we follow **Carrer de les Roses** into open countryside to head for **Elcano** boatyard.

At the junction between the boatyard and a vivid pink house, we continue straight ahead on a farm track. When the track swings left into a private house, we continue on a rougher dirt track. When this track also swings left (Wp.2 15M), we bear right on a broad walking trail. The trail climbs gently at first, then more steeply as it narrows into a path, which runs into a dirt track, 150 metres from a water-hut on the **Coll de Siller** (Wp.3 25M). Seventy five metres after the *coll*, just before the second pine tree (possibly the first by the time you read this, as the first is dying), we pass a narrow cairn-marked way on our left. This is the extension. 50 metres after that, just before the track goes under the telephone cable, we take a clearer path to the left, winding across a *carritx* covered slope toward **Cala St. Vicenç**. Passing numerous cairns and a Y-junction (the two branches soon rejoin), we

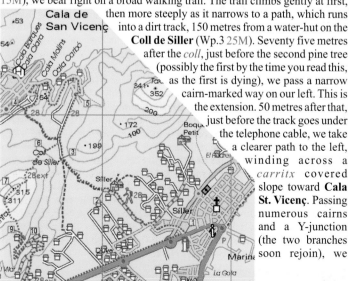

cross a shallow gully and go through a small pine wood, where the path broadens to a trail descending alongside a fence to a concrete lane (Wp.4 35M) which we follow down to a T-junction. We bear right to descend past **Hostal Los Pinos** to a second T-junction.

Cala Carbó

Bearing right again, we can either take the stairway directly into **Cala St. Vicenç** (45M) for refreshment (on the road running along the spine between **Cala Clara** and **Cala Molins** if the tourist spots nearer the beach are closed) and to visit the bronze age burial mound (further up the same road), or we can continue along the partially asphalted road toward the sea to take the 'pushchair' route back toward **Coll de Siller**.

To return to Coll de Siller. We bear right along the seafront and follow the road as it winds up the gully (which we crossed earlier) behind **Cala Carbó**. The road swings left, climbs to a modernist villa and briefly levels out. Ignoring a branch to our left, we climb again and bear right into a large roundabout, from which we take the second branch on the left (Wp.5 55M) back to **Coll de Siller** (65M).

Extension. Waypoint times are counted from the **Coll de Siller** track. Though pathless, the way is well marked with cairns and, if you look up toward the unnamed 315 metre summit (a wonderful wild little spot with excellent views), the climb behind the easternmost outcrop of rock and then directly up onto the summit is fairly obvious.

Leaving the track at the second-maybe-first pine (see above), we cross a low wall and follow a line of fencing posts (W). 30 metres from the western end of the fencing posts, we find a second cairn (Wp.6 3M), where we bear slightly left and head for the ridge. During the climb you'll be too busy watching where you put your feet and looking for the next cairn to be reading descriptions, in any case largely superfluous on such featureless terrain, but in brief: picking our way from cairn to cairn and passing occasional dull red waymarks, we climb steadily then steeply across increasingly rough ground (WSW) before zigzagging up to scramble directly over the rocks to the large pile of stones marking the top (Wp.7 45M).

Following the ridge (W) for 150 metres, we bear sharp left on the second little top at a tall thin cairn next to a red waymark (Wp.8 50M) and head for the large boat park by the main road. Ignoring the main cairn-marked way along the ridge, we maintain a southerly direction to pass a red waymark from where we can see another cairn below us in a direct line with the marina. Bearing slightly right after this cairn, we aim for the long spur that ends in two flat-roofed concrete buildings backed by what appears to be a round reservoir (in fact a dry-stone corral). Maintaining direction (S) and always heading for the spur, we hop from rock to rock and pick our way through the *carritx*, descending steadily to another large waymarked rock (Wp.9 80M) at the top of the spur, where we join a badly overgrown broad track, zigzagging down it to the top of **El Vilar** *urbanización* (Wp.10 95M). After descending through the *urbanización* to the PM-220 (105M), we turn left for a rather dreary trudge on the main road back to **Port de Pollença** (130M).

Nothing spectacular, but a very pleasant introduction to the karst and woodlands around the **Lluc** monastery, following dirt tracks and clear paths, and visiting the famous **Camel Rock**.

2 | 3H | * | 11.5 km | 200m / 200m | ↻ | 3

* Short Version 50M (estimated) ** in **Lluc**

Stroll: to the Camel Rock and back.

Access: by car or bus

From the **Serra Tramuntana Information Centre** (Wp.1 0M), we follow the monastery access road towards the C-710, turning left after 150 metres onto **Camí Reservat** drive, and then right to go through a stone gateway marked with a red dot. After crossing the football pitch and a wooden bridge at its far left corner, we take the waymarked steps climbing steadily through a chaos of delicately fluted rock.

Camel Rock

Fifty metres after the steps give way to a dirt path, there's a *sitja* on our left flanked by a stone bench and a log rubbish bin, 5 metres before which, a signpost to the right indicates the path to 'Es Camell', three minutes away on a good path (Wp.2 10M) along with Spanish graffiti claiming it's an elephant, not a camel, and that you've got to be drunk to see it!

Continuing on the main path (N), we climb to a level junction of dirt trails, where we turn left for 'Es Pixarells'. After crossing a gentle rise, we pass two benches with fine views of the **Puigs Roig** and **Caragoler**, then zigzag into a shallow depression, passing a series of *sitjes* and rocks riddled by erosion. Bearing right then left out of the depression, we climb to the **Es Pixarells Área Recreativa**, where we take the partially concreted track up towards the C-710. Below the *Área Recreativa* noticeboard, in front of a water point, are five posted parking bays (Wp.3 40M), behind which a black-arrowed waypost indicates our path through the woods.

After passing a *sitja* and crossing a small outcrop of rock, we descend on cobbled steps <u>towards</u> the designated camping area, a flat shelf with numbered posts marking the camping slots. <u>At the bottom of the steps</u>, we turn right on a rough way climbing over rocks to a path leading into a labyrinth of rocks alongside the C-710. After passing an old red waymarking arrow, we bear left at a waypost and almost immediately find another waypost and a *sitja*. Maintaining direction, we cross two large outcrops of rock, hopefully with cairns on them, to a third tall waypost, where we bear left again on a reasonably clear stretch leading to an apparent dead-end in a small glade. Just to the right of this glade there's an electricity pylon and two cairns marking a way across the rocks to the right of the pylon, after which a clear path back to the road emerges at a gateway directly in front of the principal **Menut Área Recreativa** (Wp.4 50M).

Crossing the road and the *Área Recreativa* car-park, we go behind the main building and the barbecue hut to follow a broad, trodden way descending between picnic tables (NW) to the small parking area at the bottom of the *Área Recreativa*. Bearing right, we take a broad, gated dirt track climbing towards **Puig Tomir**. Ignoring all minor branch tracks, we stay on this track as it meanders through mixed woodland, climbing through a series of concreted sections, eventually passing between two stone pillars to join the **Camí Vell de Pollença** (see Walk 32) (Wp.5 95M). Turning right, we follow the **Camí Vell** to the **Binifaldó Education Centre**, the large farmhouse visible for the last few minutes, where we emerge on the road to the **Binifaldó** bottling plant. Turning left, we follow the road up through an S-bend until it bears left through the bottling plant gates (Wp.6 110M), where we climb over the stone/concrete stile next to the closed gates on the right.

Ignoring the dirt track after the stile, we take the narrow path on the right (signposted 'Son Amer/Lluc'), which winds through the woods for fifteen minutes before rejoining the dirt track (Wp.7 125M). Bearing right, we climb to an unnamed, unmarked *coll* and continue on the dirt track down to **Coll Pelat** (Wp.8 135M). The GR continues on the level for **Lluc via Son Amer**, but we turn sharp right on a branch track descending toward the C-710.

After an easy fifteen minute descent, we cross an immense ladder-stile over a fenced stone wall leading into the public **Menut** farm. Ignoring a branch 50 metres later, we continue straight ahead to go to the left of the farmhouse and rejoin the **Binifaldó** access lane, 250 metres from the C-710. Turning left on the C-710, we cross the road 75 metres later, just before the bend, and take a stony track (Wp.9 160M) gently descending between holm oak, olives and pine. Ignoring all subsequent branches, we follow this track for a little over fifteen minutes, rejoining the outward route at the wooden bridge behind the football field.

Despite its length, this circuit is relatively easy and only earns an exertion rating of 4 for the rock-hopping in the riverbed. The scenery is very varied, but the more remarkable variety is in what we walk in and on: roads, lanes, a paved pilgrims' way, concrete tracks, cart tracks, dirt tracks, cobbled paths, *carritx* covered ways, a limestone maze, the bed of a torrent… you name it, we walk it, excepting motorways and airport runways. The ascent on the **Camí Vell** from **Caimari** (virtually unknown compared to the more celebrated and, to my mind, less attractive Old Road between **Pollença** and **Lluc**) is easy and poses no difficulties. The descent, however, via the **Serra d'en Masot** torrent should not be undertaken in wet weather (there's little risk of flooding, but the rocks might be slippery). Pathfinding is a problem between Wps.17 & 21. Long trousers or pedal-pushers are preferable to shorts between Wps. 19 & 22. Start early to avoid the improbably large coaches that plough up and down the PM-213.

4*   5½-6H **   20 km   550m / 550m   3

*   Short Versions 3
**   Short Versions **(a)** 2h   **(b)** 4h   **(c)** 2h (all estimated)

Short Versions	**Stroll**
(a) to **Lluc via Camí Vell**, returning by bus **(b)** bus to **Lluc** and descend via **Aucanella** **(c)** bus to **Lluc**, descend via **Camí Vell** (from the *fuente* at the top of the car-park)	Though it's a dreary slog at the end of a long walk, the lane between **Caimari** and **Binibona** might make a pleasant stroll on a fresh day. The **Carrer de Binibona** starts just below the smaller church at the top of **Caimari**.

Access: on foot from **Caimari** (accessible by bus). There's a large car-park on the PM-213 at the northern end of **Caimari**. If two cars are available, you may wish to leave one at **Binibona** or the **Albellons Hotel**, thus avoiding the hot trudge along the tarmac at the end.

Camí Vell de Lluc

From the northern end of **Caimari** (Wp.1 0M), we follow the PM-213 for 400 metres to the *mirador* at the first U-bend, where the **Camí Vell de Lluc** begins (Wp.2 5M). Climbing the broad track from the *mirador*, we bear right at a Y-junction (Wp.3 15M) on stairs leading to the main road, which we parallel for a while then cross (Wp.4 25M) to climb steeply on a newly paved section of the **Camí Vell**.

After passing the **Son Canta** farmhouse, we cross the road again at a U-bend just above the **Sa Coveta Área Recreativa** (Wp.6 35M), then rejoin it 50 metres later.

After following the road for 750 metres, we turn left at a marker stone and signpost (Wp.7 45M), doubling back through green gates to take a broad track that winds above the road, passing a small, locked refuge (Wp.8 50M). The track then runs up (WNW) to the head of a valley, passing a minor branch on the right and a major branch on the left (Wp.9 60M), where we come to a long, straight, gentle climb along the partially cobbled pilgrims' way. Looking down on the valley below us (SE), the small, wooded conical mountain in the middle is the **Puig Mitja**. Our return route is on the far side of this mountain.

The track narrows on a fully cobbled stretch climbing to a natural limestone gateway (Wp.10 75M) where it levels off before passing a large new building and, 20 metres later, a massive oak tree (Wp.11 80M). A gentle descent brings us to a crossroads of dirt tracks, where we maintain direction (NW) down to the main road (Wp.12 85M), 75 metres from the **Coll de sa Bataia** petrol station and bar/restaurant, where I suggest you take any refreshment you haven't got in your backpack: the coffee's not great, but the welcome is infinitely warmer than in the bars at **Lluc**.

50 metres north of the garage, we turn right on the road to **Lluc**. The **Camí Vell** descends to the left, but unless you have a strong compulsion to light a candle or catch a bus, there's little point going down to **Lluc** itself and I suggest you stay on the main road (still marked as the PM-213, though in fact now part of the C-710) for 500 metres and, just after the first left-hand bend, take the GR-212 to the right, signposted 'Binifaldó/Pollença' (Wp.13 100M). N.B. this path joins the dirt track starting just before the bend, so you could take the dirt track immediately.

Thirty metres from the road, we bear right at a waypost and small bridge to cross a deforested area and join the dirt track from the gates. The track goes through a gap in a wall, where it narrows and starts to climb, crossing a watercourse before swinging round to join another track. Ignoring all branch

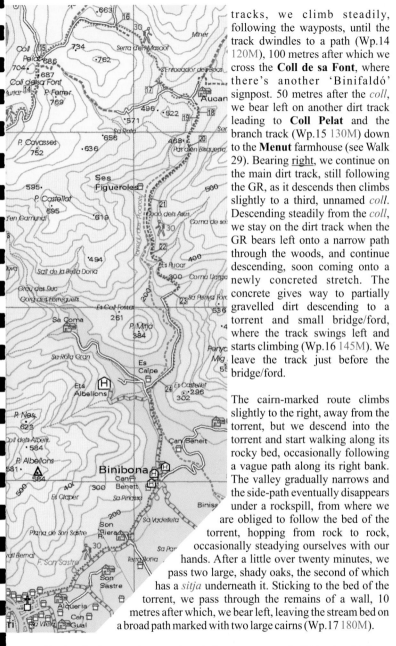

tracks, we climb steadily, following the waypoints, until the track dwindles to a path (Wp.14 120M), 100 metres after which we cross the **Coll de sa Font**, where there's another 'Binifaldó' signpost. 50 metres after the *coll*, we bear left on another dirt track leading to **Coll Pelat** and the branch track (Wp.15 130M) down to the **Menut** farmhouse (see Walk 29). Bearing right, we continue on the main dirt track, still following the GR, as it descends then climbs slightly to a third, unnamed *coll*. Descending steadily from the *coll*, we stay on the dirt track when the GR bears left onto a narrow path through the woods, and continue descending, soon coming onto a newly concreted stretch. The concrete gives way to partially gravelled dirt descending to a torrent and small bridge/ford, where the track swings left and starts climbing (Wp.16 145M). We leave the track just before the bridge/ford.

The cairn-marked route climbs slightly to the right, away from the torrent, but we descend into the torrent and start walking along its rocky bed, occasionally following a vague path along its right bank. The valley gradually narrows and the side-path eventually disappears under a rockspill, from where we are obliged to follow the bed of the torrent, hopping from rock to rock, occasionally steadying ourselves with our hands. After a little over twenty minutes, we pass two large, shady oaks, the second of which has a *sitja* underneath it. Sticking to the bed of the torrent, we pass through the remains of a wall, 10 metres after which, we bear left, leaving the stream bed on a broad path marked with two large cairns (Wp.17 180M).

One hundred metres later, we bear left on a very rough dirt track, which we leave after 50 metres, just after a short S-bend, bearing right and heading through the rocks to a line of oaks and a stone gateway (all that remains of an old wall) topped with a cairn. Going through the gateway, we wind along a natural path defined by outcrops of limestone, passing a large rock pond and crossing the rough dirt track twice, the second time beside a fragile looking waypost indicating 'Ses Figueroles/Binibona' on the right and 'Miner' on the left. Crossing the track and some low rocks, we follow a cairn-marked way winding through the rocks, bringing us down to the fenced fields of the recently restored **Aucanella** farmhouse, invisible at present but betrayed by a large bank of solar panels to our left. Pathfinding is tricky here, so follow the cairns carefully.

Just above the fenced fields, we bear right on an infinitesimally faint track (Wp.18 200M) for 50 metres, then left to find a faint path through a wall gateway (Wp.19 203M) running alongside a ditch next to the fields. At the end of the fields, we go through another wall gateway (Wp.20 207M) and bear left to cross the head of the **Torrent des Picarols** onto a faint path densely overgrown with *carritx* (watch out for concealed rocks). Passing behind a 5 metre high boulder, we bear right (S), staying on the level for about 100 metres, after which the path gradually starts to descend, passing occasional cairns.

The path passes a large stand of oaks (clearly visible from the top of the torrent), then runs alongside an old wall, before bearing away from the wall at a second stand of oaks and descending to a broader, clearer path (Wp.21 230M), about 250 metres south of the **Ses Figueroles** house, visible through much of the descent. The clear path passes two gateways before climbing gently to a three-bar gate, 50 metres after which we come to a rocky pass (Wp.22 245M) where the views open up round the conical **Puig Mitja**. Bearing left (E), we zigzag down a rocky path before bearing right (S) on a slightly overgrown stretch for a final brief climb above the **Picarols** gorge. We then resume our descent, passing a blessedly shady stretch before joining a badly eroded cart track (Wp.23 265M).

We bear right, then left 100 metres later, where cairns mark a shortcut through the woods, rejoining the track on a better stabilised section. We now stick to the dirt track as it runs alongside the torrent, passing two lime-kilns before descending toward the torrent. Just before the track starts climbing, we turn right past two large cairns (Wp.24 285M) to cross the bed of the torrent. Taking a broad path on the other side, we go through a bedstead gate, then cross an affluent onto a cairn-marked path up to the partially asphalted access track to **Sa Coma**.

Turning left, we join a tarmac lane next to the driveway to the **Albellons Hotel**, a little under ten minutes from the implausibly tidy hamlet (virtually all hotels) of **Binibona**. Ignoring the main road out of **Binibona**, we take the **Carrer de Caimari/Camí de Binibona** for a rather wearisome trudge along (and sometimes up!) the road back to **Caimari** (320M).

Puig Tomir is not the most distinctive of Mallorca's summits, but does enjoy a unique perspective on **Pollença** and the **Formentor** peninsula. More importantly, the way up is a glorious, rough little climb with a distinctly Pyrenean feel to it. Add to that a leisurely descent and long loop through remote countryside, and you've got an offer you can't refuse. Don't be deceived by the brevity of the ascent, though. Although easy, it is a steep climb on rough ground and should not be undertaken by unaccompanied inexperienced walkers. Long trousers preferable between Wps.11 & 13.

	650m
5	4¼-5H *	13 km	⌃⌄	650m	↻	⑂ ⑤ 0

* Short Versions   **(a)** 2h   **(b)** 1h40

	Short Versions
Extension From **Lluc** or **Menut** if Wp.1 is inaccessible (see text)	**(a)** if you don't mind the steep descent, return from the summit by the same route **(b)** from Wp.1 climb over the stone stile on your right and, ignoring the GR-path, follow the dirt track down till it bears sharp right at a concrete bridge/ford, Wp.16 of Walk 30. Follow Walk 30 till after Wp.17 where it emerges on the new track, joining this itinerary at Wp.14.

Access: by car or (starting from **Lluc** or the C-710) bus (seasonal timetable)

We start from the gates of the **Binifaldó** bottling plant at the **Coll des Pedregaret** (Wp.1 0M) 2.9 km from the C-710. NOTE: the main gates on the C-710 are closed at weekends. If doing this walk at the weekend or arriving by bus, you can reach Wp.1 by any of the following four options:
(i) walk up the access road from km 17.4 of the C-710 (quickest option);
(ii) follow the GR-212 from **Lluc** (most logical for the return);
(iii) follow Walk 29 from Lluc (longest and most attractive);
(iv) follow Walk 29 from the *Menut Área Recreativa* (Wp.4 of Walk 29) (short and attractive).

Taking the path to the right of the bottling plant gates, we climb alongside the fence before bearing right for a steeper climb through the woods, following cairns and red waymarks. Above the woods, we cross a scree-filled gully (Wp.2 15M) and descend briefly before climbing to traverse the head of a broader scree slope. At the north-eastern tip of the scree slope, we bear right up a second narrow gully, passing a steel cable set in the rock as a handrail, and emerging midway along another scree-filled gully (Wp3 30M). After climbing straight up this third gully, we scramble up a 5 metre high rockface (Wp.4 40M) with the help of two metal hoops and another steel cable - if this sounds alarming, bear in mind it has been tested in accordance with The Old English Sheepdog Trial (see Walk 22). We then follow a long curving valley for 50 metres before bearing right on a cairn-marked path climbing to a clear breach in the rock defining the valley.

After the breach, we continue climbing (SE) for 150 metres, following cairns onto the ridge (55M) from where we have clear views of the southern plain and **Alcúdia Bay**. Bearing left (another path on the left lower down can also be taken), we follow the ridge (NE) soon coming into view of the summit and its trig point (NOT the small summit with a pole at the top of the curving valley). Following the cairns across largely pathless limestone brings us back into sight of **Puigs Roig** and **Caragoler de Femenia** on our left (Wp.5 65M), after which a gentle climb on rough ground leads to the summit (Wp.6 75M) from where we have superb views down the **Pollença** valley. Behind **Pollença**, the first small hump is **Serra de la Coma**, the sharp peak is the **Cuculla de Fartatrix**, and the large block-like mountain below us is **Puig de Ca**, our next objective.

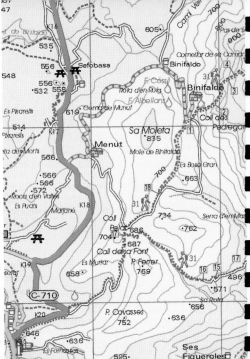

Puig Tomir

First though, we descend to the **Casa Neu** or **Snow House**, clearly visible to the south-east, where there is a grassy windbreak tucked behind the snow-gatherers' cabin (Wp.7 80M). Beyond the cabin there's a splendid snow-pit, 20 metres to the right of which, a red arrow and cairns indicate our way down. Following the cairns, red dots and occasional stretches of path, we descend in a south-easterly direction before bearing left (NNE).

A steady descent leads to a large grey metal post (Wp.8 100M) where we leave the clear trail and turn sharp right, following the cairns to scramble down onto the western limit of the **Coll del Puig de Ca**. Crossing the *coll* (E) we join a faint track (Wp.9 115M) near the wall climbing from the far side of the *coll* to the *puig*.

Turning right, we follow the track over a grassy rise, where it starts descending, skirting the fenced depression of **Clot Fondo** and running into a better-stabilised, partially concreted track down to the **Coll de l'Arena** junction (Wp.10 135M), visible for most of our descent from Wp.9. Bearing right, we follow the main track across the broad plain of **Camp Redo**. When the track ends in a turning circle (Wp.11 145M), we head for a large ladder-stile and a gap in the fence. Beyond the fence, a narrow path winds through large clumps of *carritx* (SW) passing occasional cairns and crossing the odd outcrop of rock, making its way to the head of a narrow valley (Wp.12 165M),

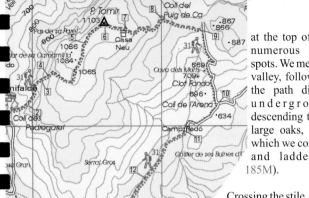

at the top of which there are numerous pleasant picnic spots. We meander through the valley, following cairns when the path disappears in the undergrowth, before descending to pass under two large oaks, 100 metres after which we come to a new fence and ladder-stile (Wp.13 185M).

Crossing the stile, we follow a broad stony trail leading to a dirt track behind the **Aucanella** (AKA **Alcanella**) farmhouse (invisible on this route).

Bearing right, we follow the track, crossing another new fence and stile, 100 metres after which we cross the signposted path taken in Walk 30. We can either follow the signposts or continue along the track as it winds round to a flat area with a ruined shelter sandwiched between the rocks on our left. Leaving the flat area, the track climbs slightly through an S-bend, just after which there's a large oak (Wp.14 200M), under which cairns and waymarks indicate the path into the torrent used in Walk 29. We can return to **Binifaldó** via the torrent (climbing to the right when we emerge on the dirt track at its head), but for a less strenuous option, we stay on the dirt track and cross the stream.

The track we're following is new and subject to litigation as it has destroyed much of an old natural 'way', so there maybe changes in the ongoing route (notably after Wp.16) according to what happens in the courts. For the present, you can either just follow the dirt track (which soon becomes more of a rubble track), or cut out several bends by taking stretches of the old 'way' marked with cairns, the first of which is 30 metres after the stream, the second (Wp.15 210M) just after a chicane climbing past the first large oak. In either case, we climb steadily till (at the time of writing!) the track ends (Wp.16 215M).

Bearing slightly left, we take a broad way (clearly the intended onward route for the track) climbing to a wall layered with rusty barbed wire. Following the wall and ignoring two branches on the right (one not very obvious), we dip down into the next valley where we climb gently through the woods, initially on an old charcoal burners' trail passing *sitjes*, then on a broad stony track, and finally on a steeper dirt track leading to a junction with a broad path (on the left) marked by a large pyramid of stones (Wp.17 230M), which is where we join the GR-212, just north of **Coll de sa Font**.

Those returning to **Lluc**, should turn left on this path and follow the GR back to **Lluc**. The rest of us stay on the main dirt track and follow the GR back to **Binifaldó**, passing **Coll Pelat** and descending from the nameless *coll* a couple of hundred metres later, finally taking the GR-wayposted branch path (Wp.18 240M) through the woods to our starting point (255M).

Six kilometres of tarmac doesn't exactly sound like a barrel of laughs, yet this descent on the **Carretera Vella** or 'old road' between **Lluc** and **Pollença** is a popular classic, passing through lovely woodland with fine picnic spots. Four of the tarmac kilometres follow quiet country lanes and the views are *said* to be good, though I can't vouch for this as the day we did this walk the clouds were about six inches off the ground.

To avoid the least attractive stretch of road walking, arrange to be picked up at km5.3 of the C-710. If you have two cars, you could just do the best bit between Wps.1&5. If you only have one car, you could start from Wp.5, do the first part of the walk in reverse, and return via the dirt track marked with red arrows. To reach Wp.5 by car, take the GR-signposted lane at km5.3 of the C-710 and park next to the **Es Clotal** gates, just before the tarmac gives way to paving, a few minutes walk from Wp.5. If arriving by bus, you can join this walk by following Walk 29 from **Lluc** or from the **Menut Área Recreativa**.

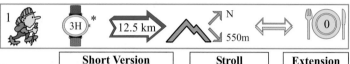

1	3H *	12.5 km N 550m ⬌ 🍴 0

* one-way

Short Version	**Stroll**	**Extension**
From Wp.5 in reverse (see introductory note)	To the picnic spot after Wp.2	Walk 29 Wps. 1-5

Access: by car or bus (seasonal timetable).

From **Binifaldó** Education Centre, we take the stony track (E) for **Pollença** (Wp.1 0M), soon passing a branch on the left (Wp.5 of Walk 29). After fifteen minutes, we go through a gate prohibiting motorbikes and bicycles, and start descending, ignoring several branch tracks. Just after a long left-hand bend, we bear right on a narrow, wayposted path (Wp.2 25M) which soon broadens to a partially cobbled trail, descending to an idyllic picnic spot beside a spring. Fifty metres below the spring, we rejoin the track.

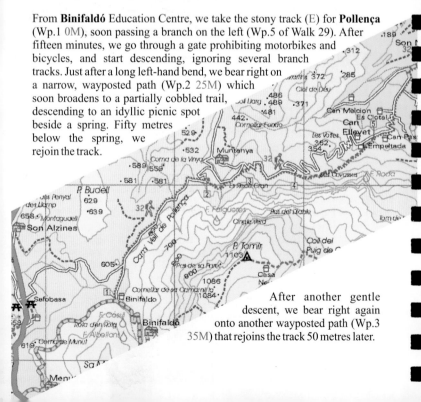

After another gentle descent, we bear right again onto another wayposted path (Wp.3 35M) that rejoins the track 50 metres later.

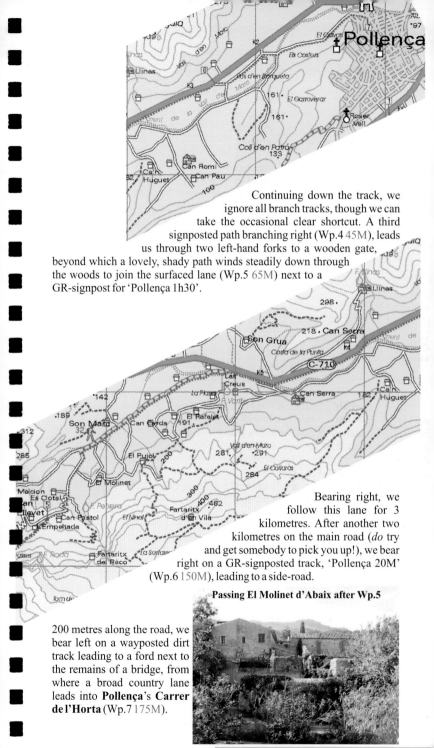

Continuing down the track, we ignore all branch tracks, though we can take the occasional clear shortcut. A third signposted path branching right (Wp.4 45M), leads us through two left-hand forks to a wooden gate, beyond which a lovely, shady path winds steadily down through the woods to join the surfaced lane (Wp.5 65M) next to a GR-signpost for 'Pollença 1h30'.

Bearing right, we follow this lane for 3 kilometres. After another two kilometres on the main road (*do* try and get somebody to pick you up!), we bear right on a GR-signposted track, 'Pollença 20M' (Wp.6 150M), leading to a side-road.

Passing El Molinet d'Abaix after Wp.5

200 metres along the road, we bear left on a wayposted dirt track leading to a ford next to the remains of a bridge, from where a broad country lane leads into **Pollença**'s **Carrer de l'Horta** (Wp.7 175M).

Puig de María

Don't be fooled by the insignificant looking little squiggle representing this walk on the map, nor by the fact that most of it is on a road. This is a glorious little excursion, ideal on a blustery winter's day when it would be unwise to tackle a wilder landscape. Our objective is the **Santuari de la Mare de Deu des Puig**, home to various religious houses from 1348 to 1988 and nowadays a bar-restaurant-refuge.

3 | 1H 10M * | 4 km | | 300m / 300m | | 5

Access: on foot from **Pollença**.

* return, + 30M for exploring

We start at km 52 of the PM-220, also the **Pollença** by-pass, on a tarmac lane signposted 'Puig de Maria' (Wp.1 0M). If starting on foot from **Pollença**, find the Repsol petrol station (signposted throughout the town as 'Benzinera'), then take the cul-de-sac to the right of the Renault concession and cut across the wasteland onto a lane that leads to a derelict house in front of Wp.1. Following the tarmac lane, we bear right after 100 metres, from where we already have fine views of the higher mountains behind **Pollença**. After climbing steadily for ten minutes, the tarmac gives way to concrete and we pass the green gates of the last house. Ignoring the water-erosion 'shortcuts' (the road is steep enough), we continue climbing through mixed woodland, passing occasional red crosses daubed on the trees - waymarks for pilgrims, not walkers.

The road ends (Wp.2 25M) in a tiny turning circle (room for three small cars, but usually full) and we continue on the restored, neatly cobbled, donkey trail with fine views south towards **Puig de Sant Martí** (see Walk 41). One hundred metres before the sanctuary, we ignore a signposted turning to the left (our return route). At the sanctuary, we can either bear right to go directly to the chapel or continue left of the main walls and go through its *Área Recreativa* (Wp.3 35M) to the impressive refectory. In either case, it's worth spending half an hour exploring. For once, what man has done with it is as magnificent and harmonious as the site: this is no dank cell for a solitary anchorite, nor an intimidating symbol of authority, but a superbly designed, well-proportioned building that once housed up to seventy people. A drink in the bar is almost compulsory. Taking the path to the left of the *Área Recreativa*, the **Camí dels Ermitans**, we visit the ruined *torre* (**Mirador de Coll Vell**) and the fenced grotto (**Avenc del Mare de Deu**), before circling back to rejoin the donkey trail for our descent.

The wild land behind the **Mortitx** estate is justly celebrated for the descent to **Rafal d'Ariant** (see Walk 35), yet **l'Havanor**, also known as **Lavanor**, rarely appears in books, which is crazy because it's a gem: easy-walking, wild terrain, and one of the most isolated and peaceful spots on the island. Access is restricted between April and May due to the Black Vulture breeding programme.

* + 15-30M for the extension, Short Version 1h25 return

Short Version	**Stroll**	**Extension**
To **Torrent de Comes**.	Past Wp.2 until the track starts to climb and back.	Down to the viewing point over **Rafal d'Ariant.**

Access: by car or bus (request stop). Park by the road 50 metres below the farm gates.

The Mortitx estate

From the **Mortitx** gates (Wp.1 0M), km 10.8 of the C-710, we follow the main farm track, crossing a cow gate and passing the farmhouse driveway. Behind the tennis courts, we ignore a waymarked branch on the right and follow the main track down to a large farm building.

Bearing right, we descend to a Y-junction at the head of a vineyard forested with trellis wires, where we bear right again. We now follow this track all the way to the end.

At the end of the vineyard, we cross a stile into the IBANAT administered area (Wp.2 15M) where we meander through groves of ancient olive trees. After a long, concreted, double S-bend, we pass a mossy track on the left. 100 metres later, just before a second gate, a track on the left (Wp.3 35M) climbs to the upper dam (Short Version Wp.4 45M) on the **Torrent de Comes**.

Continuing through the gate, we cross the lower dam's wall. Climbing steadily past wonderful rock formations, we pass a branch on the right down to the small **L'Havanor** house (Wp.5 50M excluding the climb to the upper dam). After a metalled stretch where the mesh reinforcement is exposed under worn concrete, the track narrows and continues climbing gently before levelling off above the **L'Havanor** house. We then descend into a depression with a field on our right, before passing through a gate for the final climb to the **Coll d'es Vent**, where the track bears sharp left and starts to descend within sight of the long field where it ends.

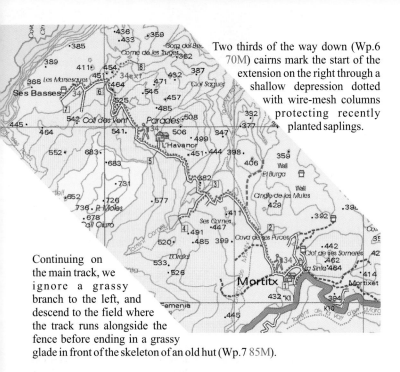

Two thirds of the way down (Wp.6 70M) cairns mark the start of the extension on the right through a shallow depression dotted with wire-mesh columns protecting recently planted saplings.

Continuing on the main track, we ignore a grassy branch to the left, and descend to the field where the track runs alongside the fence before ending in a grassy glade in front of the skeleton of an old hut (Wp.7 85M).

We return by the same route.

Extension

Pathless, but relatively easy going and reasonably well marked with cairns. Picking our way from cairn to cairn, we descend through the depression (E) till we can see the **Rafal d'Ariant** farmhouse (Wp.8 10M) and views along the coast that are just too good for the trifling approximation of words. Cairns appear to mark a way down to the **Torrent Fondo de Mortitx** (see Walk 35), but I don't recommend trying to link the two routes. We return by the same route.

This is the famous twin of the preceding itinerary, a descent into the wild, untenanted land around the abandoned **Rafal d'Ariant** farmhouse. Pathfinding is difficult and the looped return via the **Mortitx Gorge** is only for the adventurous. If you're short of time and value views over sweat sodden T-shirts and hard walking, Walk 34 is a better bet. If you want to be in the heart of the wilderness, this is the walk for you. If you have time for both, the two itineraries complement each other and are both highly recommended

* linear, 5 if returning via the gorge
** + 1h for exploring the **Ariant** estate, Short Version 2h20 (U)

Extensions: see text.

Stroll
Take the **l'Havanor** track and turn right at Wp.15 (look for a cairn on the right 5 minutes after Wp.2 of Walk 34) to the head of the gorge.

Access: by car or bus (request stop).

We start from the **Mortitx** farm gates (Wp.1 0M) as per Walk 34. Behind the tennis courts, we ignore a first turning on the right to a tiny bungalow, and take the second right passing a waymarked hut. The track descends between former cherry orchards (most of the trees have recently been uprooted) before veering right then left through a wall - if this is blocked, there's a stile just after the track veers right. We then bear left at a Y-junction and leave the track 30 metres later, turning right on a stony path (Wp.2 10M) badly overgrown with *carritx*. GPS owners who have been mocked as gadget-geeks, can now have their revenge: most of the waypoints on the outward route, are for you.

Winding through the *carritx* and picking our way over outcrops of rock, we pass occasional waymarks and cairns, descending into a large depression dotted with pine trees. If you intend coming back the same way, it's worth glancing back every once in a while to orient yourself for the return. After a gradual descent, we cross a broken fence beside a stile (Wp.3 20M) and continue on a slightly clearer path alongside the fence. Ignoring branches to the right, we cross a low stone retaining wall (Wp.4 25M) and continue alongside the remains of the fence. We then cross another wall, either by a high stile or through a broken gate on the left (Wp.5 30M) into the **Ariant** estate.

Maintaining direction (NNE), we climb through the rocks directly ahead of the stile, where there's a red waymark. Following occasional cairns and waymarks, and even more occasional stretches of clear path, we continue winding through the *carritx* and rocks (NE), and start descending through a <u>very</u> overgrown stretch - though given the prevailing invasion of *carritx*, it would be simpler to distinguish the 'undergrown' patches. If you haven't got a GPS, look for the cairns. In a landscape of rocks and rocks and rocks, and *carritx* and *carritx* and *carritx*, cairns are a better guide than words.

Rough walking, occasionally using our hands to lower ourselves between rocks, brings us down to what appears to be a natural descent off to the left. It may be natural, but it ain't for us. We climb to the right, as indicated by blue and yellow waymarks on a large cairn-topped rock (Wp.6 45M), maintaining our general direction (NNE) for 50 metres before bearing left (NNW) up a rocky escarpment to a large cairn on a broad, flat rock. Continuing on the level, we pass above a shallow depression and another natural-not-for-us descent to the left.

Maintaining direction (ENE), we climb above the depression (Wp.7 55M) and briefly follow a very faint path before climbing steeply (NNE) up a rocky watershed to a yellow arrow, where we bear left onto a *coll* with clear views of the sea (Wp.8 60M).

The way becomes slightly clearer as we descend to cross what must once have been a small lagoon and is now a *carritx* covered cirque. Winding through the *carritx*, we climb briefly before resuming our descent and coming into view of the **Rafal d'Ariant** plain. After passing an old sign for 'Mortitx', we bear left and descend steeply, soon coming into view of the **Rafal d'Ariant** farmhouse. We then zigzag down below marvellously eroded cliffs to the house (Wp.9 90M).

There are at least four extensions possible from the farmhouse:

(1) peeking over the cliffs to the north (quite sickening if you suffer from vertigo);
(2) peering into the mouth of the **Cova de ses Buixes**, or **Witches' Cave**, which is the standard end to this walk;
(3) descending for a bathe (when the water's calm) at the **Caleta d'Ariant**; or
(4) in fine weather, exploring the **Torrent Fondo de Mortitx**, which is the start of the alternative return via the gorge.

For the first three, we take the clearly visible but occasionally overgrown path to the east of the house down to a small spring with an arched roof. After the spring, we head for the **Musclo de ses Cordes**, the massive cave-riddled bluff to the north-east, crossing two walls and the dry bed of the torrent.

... dramatic views en route ...

(1) To peek over the cliffs (15M return from the house), we leave the path 100 metres after the torrent and bear left, crossing flat pathless land to the rock shelf where the torrent used to spill into a waterfall.

(2) For the cave and the cove, we stay on the path to cross a broad pass behind the **Musclo de ses Cordes**. The path descends a shallow gully of reddish-brown rocks, passing a large rock, walled-in as a makeshift shelter (easily missed on the descent). Five metres before a massive overhanging rock with a partial wall (Wp.10 a little over fifteen minutes from the house), cairns mark a faint way across the rocks to the left, at the end of which (10M return from Wp.10) a shelf over a precipitous drop gives us a view of the entrance to the **Witches' Cave**.

(3) For the cove (15M return from Wp.10), we continue past the overhanging rock and follow the cairns for a very rough descent down to the *caleta*. <u>Do not swim here if there's a swell</u>. This extension is only for those who will do anything for a swim: it's a rough descent onto sharp volcanic rock that's murder on bare feet, though there's a nice ledge for rock bathing.

(4) To explore the **Torrent Fondo de Mortitx** and start the alternative return; take the rough path to the south-west of the house, passing a series of dead fig trees and running alongside a dry watercourse. Shortly after two large pine trees, we come to the torrent where there are various waymarks (Wp.11, 5M from the house). 100 metres to the right, under a tower of rock, a series of shallow pools lead up to one deep, permanent pool. Unfortunately, it's not really swimmable as access is difficult and the water's a bit scummy. Either return the same way or take the…

Alternative return
Rafal d'Ariant is wild; the **Mortitx Gorge** is very, very wild and potentially very dangerous. There's no path, just lots of energetic scrambling. Only recommended for those who are happy without any sign of civilisation apart from intermittent cairns and waymarks. <u>Do not venture into the gorge after rain or if there's a risk of rain</u>. <u>Do tell somebody where you're going</u>.

Turning left at Wp.11 (0M), we follow the riverbed, hopping and scrambling from rock to rock. As we climb across a rock slope to the right of a first pool, the gorge starts to narrow and deepen. After ten minutes, we come to a second pool, where we either have to get wet or gingerly edge our way across the shelving rock on the

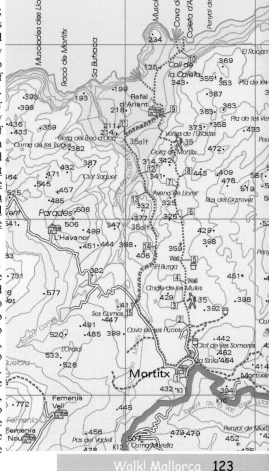

left. Less than two minutes after this second pool, we have a choice; our only one of the ascent so don't mess it up or you'll get into hellish difficulties further up! At an obvious fork in the gorge, we take the cairn and waymarked affluent to the left (Wp.12 12M).

Having made the correct choice, we hop from rock to rock up the affluent, absolved of responsibility for pathfinding – almost. After a particularly wild and narrow stretch where we have to constantly lever ourselves up with our hands between rocks, we come to a red waymark and yellow painted '30' mins (Wp.13 25M). Ignoring a rough path climbing towards a cave on the left, we carry straight on towards a cairn, after which a bilious green waymark indicates the onward route along the watercourse. The gorge gradually widens between towering rock pinnacles and we pass the occasional comforting cairn – it's not that you can get lost, but it's nice to know somebody's been here before you.

After an exhausting scramble, the gorge opens out into a natural sloping amphitheatre (40M). Following a faint path bearing right, we climb to the amphitheatre's southern 'gate', a massive rock with cliffs towering on either side (Wp.14 50M). To the left of the rock, a rough path and a final rocky stretch bring us to the base of a cliff, where we bear right on a clear path leading out of the gorge. Crossing a broken fence (60M), we stroll along a level dirt path that soon crosses a dry torrent, almost immediately after which we go through an olive grove to join the l'Havanor dirt track (Wp.15 65M). Turning left, we follow this track back past the **Mortitx** vineyard and farm buildings to the start of the walk (85M).

The **Bóquer Valley** is a bird watcher's paradise, but most visitors are lured by its unspoiled beauty and a walk that's suitable for all but the most resolutely sedentary holidaymakers. It can be crowded, but it's no less beautiful for that, and if it's solitude you're after, take the extension - nobody's going to be following you up there!

The Bóquer Valley

The mass migration of birds begins in April, but there are notable sightings for 'twitchers' all year round, in particular the rare Audouin Gull, which is found only in the Balearics and Turkey.

N.B. Some walkers have informed us that there is a gate that may be locked on the route near the farmhouse after Wp.1 due to a land dispute, which some have avoided by climbing a couple of low walls onto and off the adjacent property. It is hoped that the dispute may be solved by the time you attempt this route, but if you do experience problems of access it is best to turn back - you will have invested only a few minutes walking time at this point.

2*	1½-2H **	6 km	160m *** 160m	0

*   Short Version 1, Extension 5
**   + 1h05 for the extension, Short Version 1h-1h15
***   Short Version 80 metres, Extension + 270 metres

Short Version To **Coll del Moro**	**Stroll** To Wp.2, returning via the alternative path.	**Additional stroll** The **Bosquet de Bóquer**, 300 metres from Wp.1 along the **Formentor** road.	**Extension Cavall Bernat** (see text)

Access: on foot from **Port de Pollença**

To reach the start on foot, we follow **Port de Pollença** esplanade (NNE) to the **Restaurante Los Pescadores** and turn left on **Avenguda de Bocchoris**, crossing **Carrer de Formentor** to a pine and tamarisk-flanked promenade, the **Área Pública Bóquer, Camí de Bóquer** (Wp.1 0M) (opposite the Monte Carlo Supermarket on the **Formentor** road if arriving by car).

At the end of the **Camí de Bóquer**, formerly the driveway to the **Bóquer** farm (the castellated building ahead of us), we cross two new roads and take the **Predio Bóquer** track up to the farm gates, where we are greeted by the customary catalogue of prohibitions.

Going through the main gates, we pass in front of the house, go through a

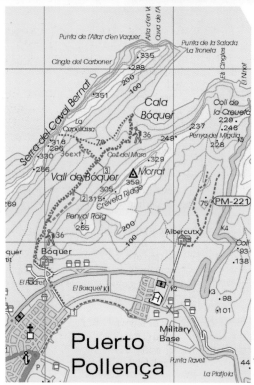

second gate, and bear right through a third gate (the Mallorcans do love a good gate!), after which we follow the broad path climbing gently between the **Serra del Cavall Bernat** and the **Creveta Ridge**.

Going through a narrow defile formed by two pinnacles of rock, we pass a lime-kiln within sight of a small stand of pine, after which the valley broadens and the outline of the bay becomes clearer. The path crosses a stone wall (Wp.2 20M), just before which a branch track doubles back on the right.

Up to our left, we can see one of the 'eyes' through the **Cavall Bernat**. The shallow dip in the ridge to the right of the eye is **La Capellassa**, our objective on the extension.

For the present though, we continue towards the sea and, five minutes later, reach a branch path on the left (Wp.3 25M) marked by a large cairn. This is the extension.

If you're not doing the extension
Stay on the main path for another five minutes to the **Coll del Moro**, identifiable by a large pile of stones.

For the short version
Stop at the *coll* and return via the same route or the alternative stroll.

For the full version
Bear right at the *coll* and follow the cairns down the valley along a wide path that reaches the beach fifteen minutes later. The beach itself isn't up to much, stony, speckled with patches of tar, and strewn with piles of flotsam, but the bay is unspoilt and the water's good for swimming in fine weather, though hazardous in rough seas due to the rocks and debris.

Extension
The scramble up to **La Capellassa** on the **Cavall Bernat** is nigh on indescribable, but if you've got sturdy legs and a hunger for stunning views, it's a must. Turning left at Wp.2, we descend a rough but clear path beside a

stone wall, at the end of which we start climbing. The path becomes increasingly difficult to distinguish from other patches of bare ground, but following the cairns we climb to the right of a smooth outcrop of rock. The cairns are confusing here, so bear in mind you're not going anywhere specific and where you are going is up all the way!

As we near **La Capellassa**, the path clears briefly before disappearing again. In the last 50 metres, various routes splinter off from one another, the main cairn-marked route bearing left toward the **Cavall Bernat** proper. It is possible to follow the ridge all the way to **Cala St. Vicenç**, but this is notoriously difficult and not recommended. Instead, we bear right, straight up a pathless slope aiming for the lowest point on the ridge. But don't hurry. There's a sheer drop on the far side and it's not one to confront suddenly. If the route up was indescribable, so are the views from the top, taking in the jagged grandeur of **Formentor** to the east and toe-curling cliffs to the west.

A forty minute climb is followed by a twenty-five minute descent along the same route, picking our way from cairn to cairn with extreme caution since it's very unstable underfoot. However, instead of bearing right towards Wp.3, we bear left halfway down to follow goat paths towards the bay, emerging 50 metres north-west of **Coll del Moro** on a minor path, where we bear left for a gentle descent to a boulder-strewn watercourse leading to the beach.

To return, we climb between the remains of old walls 10 metres east of the watercourse. Joining the main cairn-marked path, we wind up the eastern side of the valley, passing ancient terracing walls and an old *canaleta* outlet, reaching the **Coll del Moro** fifteen minutes later.

For a slight variation on the return and for the stroll

Bear left at Wp.2 (5M from **Coll del Moro**) on a broad track climbing slightly towards **Penyal Roig**. The track flattens out and dwindles to a path in front of a concrete hut with a green door, before dropping down below a narrow stone-capped *canaleta* to rejoin the outward route just short of the defile.

37 CREEK & PEAK 1 - NA BLANCA from FORMENTOR

Cap Formentor doesn't have a great reputation for walking, as its sheer cliffs and rough rocks can seem a little daunting when seen from the road. And if the mania for fencing continues apace, this sorry reputation will become sorrier still, which is a pity because there are some excellent walks in the area, as these Creek & Peak combinations are designed to illustrate. The traditional circuit of **Na Blanca** has been blocked near the main **Formentor** car-park and, at the time of writing, one version of the southern ascent is overgrown. However, the main route is still passable. It's tough walking over rough virtually pathless terrain and, though it's carefully marked with cairns, you need reasonable pathfinding skills. But the views from the top are worth the effort: 'limpid blue waters', 'dramatic crags', 'fabulous vistas' – you trundle them out, the clichés all fit.

N.B. Thir route is not recommended after heavy rains as the 'path' at Wp.2, already a scramble, becomes a watercourse, making it difficult to negotiate.

| 4 | 2½ H | 10 km | 340m / 340m | ⟷ | 3 |

* at **Playa Formentor**

Stroll	Additional Stroll
Along the beach to 'the poets'.	From the **Mirador d'es Colomer** on the PM-221 to the **Albercutx** watchtower (also possible by car).

From the small car-park directly behind **Formentor** beach (Wp.1 0M), we cross the restaurant terrace and stroll along the beach for ten minutes, passing below the long, low white buildings of the hotel. Approaching **Illa de Formentor**, we climb onto a large turning circle in front of the **Club de los Poetas**, which despite the name and uniformed maid, is not a club and probably has very little to do with poetry, either.

Following the road inland, we pass a branch to the right and the deliriously pompous **Castillo del Mar**, after which the road bears sharp left round the hotel tennis courts, and we continue on a lane off to the right marked with a dead-end sign.

Na Blanca

We follow this lane through successive tarmac and concrete sections until it ends at the green gates of the last house, on the left of which a red waymark indicates the start of our scramble up to **Na Blanca** (Wp.2 30M).

Guided by cairns and the occasional waymarks, we zigzag up to join the remains of an old path climbing the ridge (NNE) from a gate at the back of the house.

After twenty minutes, the path loses what little definition it had and we follow the cairns, climbing steadily through scattered pine and dwarf palm with increasingly fine views to the east.

Illa de Formentor

As the gradient eases, we bear WNW, picking our way across jagged debris within sight of the white rocks of the peak, which is in fact still surprisingly far away. Although the way seems simple, keep following the cairns as this is very rough walking and the marked route has not been chosen by accident. Halfway along this westerly ridge, beware of cairns indicating a way to the right. We maintain direction to skirt the cliffs overlooking the hotel and finally reach the top (Wp.3 80M). The return by the same route takes about an hour, plus however long you need for bathing from the pretty little sandy beach in front of 'the poets'.

The first part of this little known itinerary, an easy stroll down to **Cala Figuera**, is suitable for a family excursion. The climb to **El Morro de Catalunya** is not, and should only be attempted by experienced walkers. It's not technically difficult, but does cross rough, pathless ground and involves picking one's way from cairn to cairn, hoping the people who built them knew what they were doing - they did, as it happens, but it's not always evident. The rewards, though, are correspondingly great as we climb into some of the wildest terrain encountered anywhere on the island and enjoy a unique view of the peninsula. Don't do it on your own, or when it's wet or very windy.

| 5 | 3-3½ H * | 8.5 km | 380m / 380m | ⇔ | 0 |

*   Short Version 1½h

Access: by car

| **Short Version** To the *coll* at Wp.3 | **Stroll** To **Cala Figuera** |

Cap Formentor

We start at km 12 of the PM-221 to **Cap Formentor**, parking next to the road just after the milepost or on a rough dirt track on the right 50 metres further along. From a gateway in the fence on the northern side of the road (Wp.1 0M), we cross a clearing to take a broad dirt track bearing right.

The track descends to a platform above the beach, where it joins our return route, the steep path down from the large parking area at km 13. Bearing left, we take the steps down to the stony beach (Wp.2 20M), which was a bit smelly when we passed, littered with the decaying corpses of tiny blue jellyfish, but there are nice rock-bathing shelves below the rock sheets along the northern side of the bay, at the end of which we can peer into a remarkable sea-cave.

For the full and short versions
We bear left at the end of the rock sheets and climb towards a clear gully, where we find a red waymark and cairned trails climbing on either side of the gully. Ignoring the cairns on the left, we cross the bottom of the gully and follow the cairns to the right, climbing alongside the rocky outcrop on the gully's left bank (our right). Edging up the rock, we pass a large uprooted pine tree and climb to the right of a second small outcrop of rock bringing us into view of the lighthouse at **Cap Formentor**. Following the cairns, we climb along a rockspill to pass behind the second outcrop of rock, back into the gully.

The cairns briefly disappear, but up to our right, a red waymark on a rock flanked by dwarf palm indicates where we cross onto the gully's right bank.

Following a route well marked with cairns, we climb steadily to the obvious *coll* north of the gully (Wp.3 55M) though strictly speaking it's not really a *coll*, since you wouldn't want to pass onto the other side, where there are almost sheer drops down to the sea.

Even if you don't intend continuing to the end, it's worth climbing to this point. The views of **Cala Figuera** and **El Fumat** are superb, while the outlook to the north would curdle milk, let alone blood.

For the full walk

We bear right at the *coll* towards another cairn and a waymark indicating that we climb straight up the steep, exposed rock just to the right of the cliffs (yes, <u>that</u> way up!). At first, there's no confirmation that this is the right route, but we soon pass two small cairns (invisible from below) and climb very steeply to a tall cairn in the pine trees at the top of the slope (Wp.4 60M).

We've now done most of the climbing, but the roughest ground and most tortuous pathfinding awaits.

Casas Velles

Beforehand though it's worth looking back inland, where the views are already opening out and we can see the green fields of **Casas Velles** and, in the distance, the **Torre de Albercutx**.

Bearing slightly left from the tall cairn, we climb for 10 metres to another cairn and the first of several red arrows that guide us along the crest. The first arrow indicates our more or less level way round the edge of the first outcrop of rock.

After 50 metres, at a cairn and waymark, we bear sharp left to climb steeply for 15 metres, after which we bear right again to resume our general north-easterly direction. Climbing gently, we pass a second red arrow, 10 metres after which a third red arrow directs us <u>downhill</u>.

Descending over large smooth rocks for 5 metres (on your bottom if necessary, this is no place for dignity), we bear left at a fourth arrow to skirt a pine tree and pass a fifth arrow indicating the way over the smooth exposed rock, beyond which we climb back towards the crest along a route marked by cairns and waymarks.

The next red arrow (Number Six if I haven't missed any) indicates a way directly over the rocks, while the cairns lead round to the right of the rocks: <u>follow the cairns</u>. Carefully picking our way round the southern side of the rocks (not dangerous, but the rocks are sharp and a fall would be very unpleasant), we rejoin the waymarked route and scramble over the rocks onto a broad ridge, which we follow for 100 metres to the large pile of stones on the top (Wp.5 95M) from where we have a matchless view of the peninsula.

We return by the same route. The descent back to the creek takes a little over an hour, after which a swim is not so much welcome as essential.

To return to the starting point
From the platform above the beach, we take the narrow, overgrown path climbing SSW. Just before the pine trees halfway up, we bear right onto another overgrown path and keep climbing (W) at each junction till the path broadens, first to a walking trail then a forest track, joining the main road five minutes from Wp.1.

Apart from the last stretch, this is an easy walk along tarmac lanes and dirt tracks. Though blighted by a big, ugly house, **Cala Murta** is an easily accessible, attractive creek with a stony beach and small picnic area. The unnamed summit enjoys fine views and is adjacent to **Na Blanca**, an extension avoiding most of the pathfinding problems of Walk 37. Though not as wild as the other creek-&-peak walks, this is a pleasant excursion with some excellent views.

*	+ 20M for the extension
**	+ 80 metres for the extension

Stroll	**Extension**
To **Cala Murta/El Castellet** and back.	To **Na Blanca** (see text).

Access: by car. Park at the large car-park at km13 of the PM-221 above **Cala Figuera**.

We start shortly before km 13 of the PM-221 at a walking sign for **Cala Murta** (Wp.1 0M) indicating the tarmac lane down to the creek. The attractive little lane winds through a profusion of *pistacia* and dwarf palms to pass a transformer tower and start its gentle descent. After passing a picnic area on our left and a first branch track on our right, we cross a small bridge over the dry torrent, just after which there is a second branch on the right (15M Wp.3), the track we follow for the full walk.

For the moment though, we continue on the tarmac lane, which ends at the gates of a private house. Bearing right on the dirt access track, we cross the beach (20M) to a signposted path west of the creek, which leads to a small *mirador* above the rocky headland at **El Castellet** (Wp.2 25M) from where we have attractive views along the coast in both directions.

Retracing our steps to the branch beside the torrent (Wp.3 35M), we take the broad dirt track running alongside the torrent. The track soon passes a *sitja* and dips down to cross an affluent just below a small dam wall, from where it bears left to climb alongside the affluent, gently at first then more steadily, until it comes to a locked gate.

In theory, this land is closed to hikers, but the owner is not one of the difficult variety. "It's closed?", we said. "Yes", he said, "it's closed". "So we can't pass?" we said. "It's closed", he said, gloomily, "but you just climb over the fence like everybody else does". So we did. A brief climb after the gate brings us to a T-junction of tracks just above **Coll del Olivares** (Wp.4 60M).

Bearing left at the T-junction, we continue climbing until the track levels off and we come to a large green fire-fighting reservoir (Wp.5 85M). The track bears left, dwindling to a broad trail and passing a line of cairns on our right

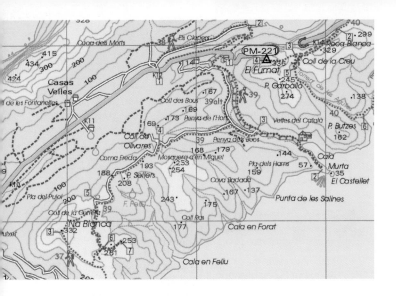

(the return route on the extension). Continuing on the trail as it skirts the south-east of **Na Blanca**, we pass several more cairns until we come to two larger cairns flanking the trail (Wp.6 95M).

We leave the trail here, turning left (SE) onto a rubble 'way' that might once have masqueraded as a track but has long since given up the unequal battle. After 75 metres, a small cairn indicates where we bear left to pick our way over sharp rocks skirting the first small top (261 metres) to cross *carritx* and dwarf palm scrubland onto the second small top (253 metres) (Wp.7 105M) from where we have fine views along the coast and into the triple gorge behind **Cala en Feliu**. Unless you wish to do the extension, return the same way except, just before the dam above Wp.3, bear left on a dirt trail to rejoin the tarmac lane a few hundred metres further up.

Extension

If you haven't already climbed **Na Blanca**, you can do so from Wp.6. Continue on the rocky trail between the two flanking cairns round the head of the **El Seller** valley. As the trail bears left on the western side of the valley, turn right on a 'way' across debris and bare rocks marked by cairns and red waymarks. Thirty metres later, bear right again to follow the cairn-marked route up to **Na Blanca** (15M from Wp.6 / see Walk 37 for a general description).

To find the cairns and waymarks down to the reservoir from **Na Blanca**, head NE, aiming between the **Morro de Catalunya** (the round pinnacle to the left) and **El Fumat** (on the right with its distinctive zigzag path), slightly favouring the **Morro**. When you see the **Casa Velles** fields, take a more easterly direction, aiming to the right of **El Fumat**. The reservoir is soon visible and all you have to do is follow the cairns along the ridge, returning to Wp.5 in roughly fifteen minutes. From here it takes about fifty minutes to return to Wp.1.

40 CREEK & PEAK 4 - EL FUMAT, TORRENT DE LES AGULLES, & CALA EN GOSSALBA

This is the ultimate Creek & Peak in every sense. **El Fumat** is well known, which isn't terribly surprising given that the road runs right through it; even sightseers who never get out of their cars and just train the camcorder on the passing scenery, will probably notice it's got a bit dark when they drive through the tunnel. **Cala en Gossalba** is also well known though surprisingly little visited.

Our descent, however, from **El Fumat** to the *cala* via the dry **Torrent de les Agulles** doesn't appear in any other guidebook I've seen, which is quite inexplicable as it's a lovely wild little walk and makes a far more satisfying circuit than the traditional scramble over **Roca Blanca**.

Despite its intimidating aspect, **El Fumat** is a relatively easy climb, and though our descent crosses rough, pathless ground, it poses no problems so long as you're sure-footed and well-shod. The complete circuit would be a good excursion for a family with venturesome adolescents. Not recommended when it's wet or very hot.

| 3 | 2H 10M * | 6 km | 340m / 340m | ↻ | 🍴 | 0 |

* Short Version 1¾ h

Short Version	Stroll
Short Version Excluding **El Fumat**	To **Cala en Gossalba** and back via our return route. The path down, which isn't immediately visible from the *mirador*, starts 10 metres before the metal crash barriers on the right (direction **Cap Formentor**).

Access: by car. Park at the small *mirador* shortly before km 15 of the PM-221. Best to get there early as there's only room for three or four cars. There's space for one car back towards the tunnel, just before the bend.

From the *mirador* (Wp.1 0M) we walk back along the road towards the tunnel, soon coming into view of **El Fumat**. 100 metres from the sign announcing the tunnel, a small cairn and an old blue arrow indicate where we scramble up off the road (Wp.2 10M) on a narrow path leading to the remains of the old donkey-trail (clearly zigzagging up to **Coll de la Creu** in the distance) formerly used to supply the lighthouse. A gentle climb along the donkey trail brings us onto the *coll* (Wp.3 25M), where we see the path zigzagging down from the pass above the **Cala Murta** valley.

N.B. It is possible to reach the *coll* via the stairs on the **Pollença** side of the tunnel: this should only be attempted by men 'super, spider, or bat', as sheer drops mean one needs to be able to fly or cling to the rock like a limpet.

At the western end of the *coll*, red waymarks and cairns indicate the way up to

El Fumat. Clear, easy walking up small patches of scree, some so well trodden it's almost a path, and sloping rock shelves, brings us to the base of the peak, where we bear left towards **Alcúdia** to follow the waymarks round the rocks to the top (Wp.4 40M).

Returning to the *coll*, we continue on the donkey trail, zigzagging down toward the head of **Torrent de les Agulles**, where there's a 50 metre level stretch, at either end of which two clear but narrow watersheds feed into the main torrent. Leaving the path at the first of these watersheds (Wp.5 55M), we descend alongside the watershed, picking our way across *carritx* covered debris. We soon come to a reassuring cairn at the crux of the two watersheds. We then follow a rough path through the *carritx*, to the junction with a second, larger watershed, where we take to the bed of the torrent.

Cala en Gossalba

And that's pretty much it. Unless you're feeling in an unusually perverse mood, you can't really get lost down here, and we just keep on keeping on down the torrent, hopping from rock to rock, skirting the occasional fallen pine, but always staying in or near the bed. The rocks get larger, the landscape wilder the lower we go, passing some superb rock formations as we approach the declivity of the *cala*. Within sight of the sea, we reach a final little rock shelf that's easily descended, though you may need to slide on your bottom for a moment, before eventually emerging on a tiny stony beach backed by crystal clear waters (Wp.6 100M).

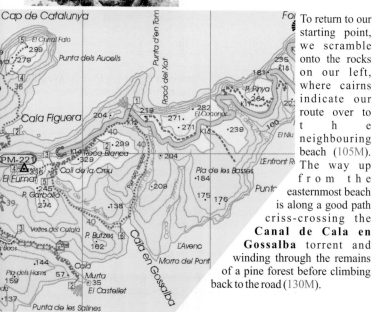

To return to our starting point, we scramble onto the rocks on our left, where cairns indicate our route over to the neighbouring beach (105M). The way up from the easternmost beach is along a good path criss-crossing the **Canal de Cala en Gossalba** torrent and winding through the remains of a pine forest before climbing back to the road (130M).

Puig Sant Martí is the singular, slightly dull looking hillock behind **Playa Alcúdia**. Don't be deceived though. It's a stiff climb with some modest pathfinding problems, and the outlook on **Alcúdia**, the **Sa Pobla** plain, and the **Tramuntana** is splendid. If you're staying in **Alcúdia**, it's a must.

4* | 1¾-2H ** | 6.5 km | 250m / 250m | ↻ | 0 ***

* Short Version 3   ** Short Version 1½h (estimated)   *** in **Playa Alcúdia**

Short Version	**Stroll**
(More precisely, an easy version) in reverse, either to the smaller peak to the north, or on the easy, pathless route to the higher peak; in either case, return the same way.	To Wp.4 in reverse

Access: by car or on foot from **Playa Alcúdia**

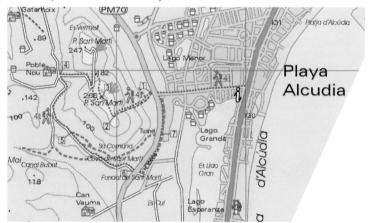

From the **Playa Alcúdia** Tourism Information Office, we follow **Avenida Pere Mas I Reus** for 800 metres to the ruby and white **Edificio Siesta** apartments beside the bypass. The original start of the steep climb to the *puig* has been obliterated by the bypass, but if you trace an imaginary line up from the *avenida*, you should be able to pick out the bare earth of the watercourse we follow to the top.

Crossing the bypass (traffic is sparse but fast, so take care) to the right of the *avenida* T-junction, we climb over the crash barrier (Wp.1 0M) to scramble up a gap in the brush (marked with a small cairn) onto a mound of dirt. Bearing left towards a small stand of pine, we cross *carritx* and exposed rock to pick up the old path climbing to the right just before the pine. Ignoring a branch on the right, we climb towards the watercourse along a rough path studded with exposed rock and boulders. The path gets rougher and more overgrown the higher we go, obliging us to weave in and out of the watercourse, rapidly gaining height to emerge on the shallow *coll* to the left of the *puig* (Wp.2 25M). To reach the summit, we bear right on a narrow 'way' winding along the ridge, passing two cairns and a pothole, before a pathless scramble over bare rock brings us to the northern tip of the *puig* (Wp.3 35M), in view of the telecommunication towers on the smaller peak to the north. From this little eyrie we have superb views through 360°.

There are two ways to descend, one quick and perilous along something approximating a path, the other more or less pathless but considerably less precipitous. Both end on the road to the telecommunication towers. Just below us, on the western side of the *puig*, is a short denuded spur with a few pine trees halfway along its back. We descend onto the upper part of this spur.

For the quick, perilous path
We bear slightly to the right on a rough path descending directly to the U-bend in the road (not for wet weather – at the best of times it's a crab-like descent and even the big rocks are unstable).

For the gentler, pathless route
We bear right <u>below</u> the limestone rocks capping the *puig* and follow the ridge to join the road 150 metres above the U-bend.

Once on the road, we bear left and stroll down to a junction in front of a gated house (Wp.4 60M). Turning left, we follow a dirt track through the woods behind the *puig*, bearing left five minutes later at a Y-junction signposted 'Cova de Sant Martí'. The dirt track climbs gently round the southern end of the *puig*, passing a cairn-marked path to the left (Wp.5 70M; for an alternative finish you can take this path, which curves round the hillside before dropping down to go through a tunnel under the bypass and emerge at Wp.7) and, 50 metres later, another track on the left. Carrying straight on at the 'Canal d'en Bubo' T-junction (75M), we soon reach a gentle descent back to the bypass (Wp.6 80M).

Beyond the bypass, our track descends towards the lagoon, passing a large green metal cross marking the enclosed **Cova de Sant Martí** grotto. Twenty metres after the *cova*, we leave the track, bearing left on a narrow path winding through wild olive and pine woods till it's sandwiched between the bypass and a newly built slab of flats; if this path has been churned up by horse riders you can continue on the track to the metalled road.

Cova de Sant Martí

Ignoring a tunnel under the bypass (Wp.7 95M), we continue towards the **Edificio Siesta**, finally coming to a second tunnel, this time under the **Avenida Pere Mas I Reus**. The path continues toward the equestrian centre 200 metres further along, but we bear right to rejoin the *avenida*.

If doing this route in reverse
At the end of the **Avenida Pere Mas I Reus**, go to the left of the crash barriers between the by-pass junction and the **Edificio Siesta**, passing a white concrete bench and a small white building fronted with a ceramic map of Mallorca, just after which you'll find the path on your left.

Despite its proximity to one of the island's largest beach resorts, the **Alcúdia Peninsula** is a surprisingly wild place, long forsaken by man apart from the aborted **Bon Aire** *urbanización*, a small golf course, and the military installations on **Cap des Pinar**. At first glance, it can seem a bit barren, but once the eyes are used to it, there's a distinct charm to the folds of the land and the rough vegetation.

Unfortunately, the only bus service stops at **Mal Pas** and only runs in summer. Using the extension, this walk gives pedestrian access to the longer tours of the **Talaia d'Alcúdia** and **Penya Roja** (see Walks 43 & 44). It also serves as a lovely introduction to the peninsula and the island's flora, passing through a profusion of nearly all Mallorca's classic shrubs: *pistacia*, euphorbia, *carritx*, asphodel, broom, dwarf palm and more.

| 2 | 1H 20M * | 7 km ** | 260m ↗ 260m ↘ | ↻ | 🍴 0 |

*   + 1h for the extension
** + 6km for the extension

| **Extension** See text. | **Stroll** As per the extension; see text. |

Access: by car and on foot from **Alcúdia**. Motorists take the **Mal Pas** road from **Alcúdia**, turn right at the **Bodega del Sol Bar**, and follow the **Camí de la Muntanya** to the end of the tarmac at the entrance of the **Victoria Área Natural**.

Extension

If you're walking from **Alcúdia**, take the side-road just south of the Repsol Petrol Station and, after 100 metres, bear right on the lane skirting **Sa Vinya**.

After another 100 metres, turn left on the **Camí S'Alou**. We then follow this attractive lane for 2 km until it joins the **Camí de la Muntanya**. The start of the walk is 500 metres on our right, where the tarmac ends at the entrance to the **Victoria Área Natural**.

The extension, from Alcúdia

From the entrance gates (Wp.1 0M), we bear left on a broad track (see picture on the next page), climbing through the trees. After a couple of minutes, we pass a path to the right signposted **Coll de ses Fontanelles** - our return route, though if you don't have a car and want to climb the **Talaia** (Walk 43) it would

The start of the main walk

be more logical to take this turning now.

Our track climbs gently then dips into a valley as it dwindles to a path with good views of **Pollença** bay.

After crossing two watercourses, we climb toward the terraced garden and large greenhouse of an enormous hilltop villa (very grand from a distance, but unfinished and apparently abandoned), behind which we have our first sight of the **Talaia**. We then descend alongside the **Bon Aire** *urbanización* amid a mass of shrubbery, passing a branch coming in from the left, after which we gradually bear right (ENE), crossing a small rise, before joining a dirt track above the **Torrent de Fontanelles** (Wp.2 25M).

Bearing right, we cross the torrent just below a tiny dam, where we leave the track and take a cairn-marked path up the torrent's right bank. This pleasant path, occasionally invaded by shrubbery, climbs gently alongside the torrent before crossing back onto the left bank, from where we can see the clump of trees at the **Coll de ses Fontanelles**.

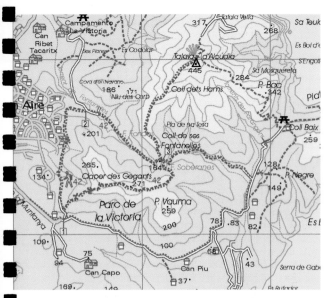

Continuing our climb, we cross the torrent three times, before a final, slightly steeper ascent, brings us to the crossroads at the *coll* (Wp.3 45M).

For a slightly longer walk, carry straight on here to follow Walk 43 in reverse to the **Camí de la Muntanya**; for a very long walk, turn left for the **Talaia** (see Walks 43 & 44); otherwise, we turn right on the path marked by a large cairn.

Climbing steadily, we cross a minor *coll* from where we can see the **Illa d'Alcanada** (S), after which a final brief climb brings us over the **Claper des Gegants** knoll, within sight of **Alcúdia**'s commercial port. The path levels out and descends very slightly to skirt another knoll, after which we gradually zigzag down (as always, much further that one would expect), traversing a fallen pine and head-high euphorbia, and detouring round another fallen pine, almost immediately after which we rejoin our outward route at the 'Coll de ses Fontanelles' sign, thirty minutes from the *coll*, and two minutes from our starting point.

The **Talaia d'Alcúdia** can be a bit of a motorway, especially on the dull, 'classic' route from the north, but it's popular with good reason, boasting excellent views, both inland and out to sea. It may seem a little perverse to drive to the end of the peninsula then walk inland, but there's method to this madness as it means we can climb to the top by the little used western ridge and (subject to the safety warning; see text) end our walk with a swim.

| 4 | 2H * | 8 km | ⟋⟍ 350m 350m | ↻ | ⍟ 0 |

* + 50M
for the
extension

Short Version/Stroll & Extension
Platja des Coll Baix - not for the fragile or very young given the hazardous rocks and currents. Don't attempt it in flip-flops, either. At the very least, stout walking sandals or trainers are required. Also an attractive destination for a bike excursion from **Alcúdia** (ask for hire details at the Tourist Information Office).

Access: by car, bike or on foot from **Alcúdia** (see Walk 42); start as per Walk 42 and continue to the end of the **Camí de la Muntanya**. Drivers stop in the large turning circle just below the **Coll Baix** chain, cyclists at the bike-rack in the *Área Recreativa*.

From the car-park/turning circle (Wp.1 0M), we walk back along the **Camí de la Muntanya** and, shortly after a chained track to the left, turn right for 'Coll de ses Fontanelles' (Wp.2 7M) on a track alongside the bed of a dry torrent. The track (bizarrely carpeted with wild broad beans!) peters out 150 metres later and we cross the dry torrent to take a clear, cairn-marked path climbing into mixed pine and wild olive.

After running alongside the torrent, the path dips down, re-crossing the torrent twice, continuing through dense *carritx* and increasingly infrequent trees. After a fourth crossing, we climb away from the torrent alongside the course of an affluent, winding round a couple of fallen pine. Cairns then lead us away from the affluent along a narrow path traversing the hillside before dipping down to cross the head of the main torrent. A brief climb brings us to the crossroads at **Coll de ses Fontanelles** (Wp.3 30M), where we turn right towards the **Talaia d'Alcúdia**, which has been visible for the last ten minutes.

Our path briefly disappears on an outcrop of rock, at the top of which we bear left, climbing steadily toward the first pronounced spine along the ridge, more of hump when you're on top of it. One minute after the hump, we bear left at a large cairn and climb steeply across a pathless outcrop of rock marked by cairns onto a slightly clearer trail (largely pioneered by

goats, but clear enough if you follow the cairns) at the base of the main spine. After a steep climb, we scramble up the natural 'steps' at the western end of the **Talaia** to the top (Wp.4 75M). There's a small refuge just below the summit.

The Talaia from Coll Baix

The onward path is visible to the south. Briefly descending by the main access path (E), we turn right for 'Platja des Coll Baix' and follow a clear stony path round to the south of the **Talaia**. We then descend steadily to the watershed between **Sa Mosquereta** and the **Torrent des Parangons**, after which a gentle climb skirts **Puig Boc**. A final steep descent, tamed by innumerable hairpin bends, brings us down to the **Coll Baix Área Recreativa** (Wp.5 115M), where we can either return directly to the car or turn left for **Platja des Coll Baix**.

Extension
Gently descending through a sickly pine wood, we ignore two branches to the left and pass a large V-trunked pine, immediately after which the path briefly divides. A third branch to the left is a shortcut, but we continue to a junction where fainter traces carry straight on and the main path turns sharp left (Wp.6, 12M from Wp.5). Following the main path, we zigzag down through the trees, ignoring another shortcut near the end, 15 metres after which the path bears left on steps down to a red arrow indicating the 'way' over the rocks. We then pick our way along the rocks, keeping an eye on the alarmingly friable agglomerate to our left. It's evident from the debris that these cliffs regularly collapse, so don't venture along here after heavy rain.

Fresh rockfalls mean this section changes frequently, but at the time of writing, a roughly beaten path over the debris makes its way under a rather disturbing overhang, before we finally hop over the remaining rocks onto the beach (Wp.7 25M). We return by the same route.

WARNING: <u>This beach is notoriously dangerous</u>. The fact that the notice forbidding swimming in rough seas is in <u>five</u> languages is not merely the consequence of a casual polyglottism down the town hall.

The undertow is strong, people drown. ONLY swim here when it's dead calm, otherwise you'll be the one that's dead calm.

44 ALCÚDIA PENINSULA 3 - TALAIA D'ALCÚDIA & PENYA ROJA

This is a testing walk with some significant pathfinding problems between Wps. 3 & 7, but it's easily broken up and, if you only have time for one walk on the peninsula, this is probably the one to do, as it's a summation of the other two, taking us up the **Talaia** and through (right through!) the flora noted in Walk 42. Long trousers are advisable. The extension is highly recommended, either as part of the main walk or as an itinerary in itself.

*	Short Versions (a) 1 (b) 4 (c) 3
**	+ 1h10 for the full extension
	Short Versions (a) 1h (b) & (c) 2h
***	+ 130 metres for the extension
****	at the *ermita*

| **Extension** **Penya Roja** and **Puig Romani**. | **Strolls** To the *mirador* at the western end of the car-park |

Short Versions

(a) to **Cova Navarro**
(b) follow the dirt track (E) from the *ermita* then take the final impressive path to the peak.
(c) as per **(b)**, but take the path on the left (Wp.8) to **Penya Roja** and **Puig Romani**.

Access: by car or bike. From **Alcúdia**, take the **Mal Pas** road and follow the *ermita* sign to the left of the **Bodega del Sol Bar**. Park at the **Restaurant/Hostal Ermita de la Victoria**.

From the start of the dirt track at the eastern end of the *ermita* car-park, we take the path on the right behind the mapboard (Wp.1 0M). The path drops down steeply before bearing right on an easier gradient and descending to cross a small bridge over the **Aladernar Torrent**.

At the Y-junction immediately after the torrent, we bear left and climb through the pine on a broad trail that soon dwindles to a shrub-lined path. The path levels out, with the **Talaia** visible to our left, before crossing two affluents of the **Aladernar**. Shortly after the second affluent, we ignore a minor path to the right, and maintain direction (W) on a dirt track, passing a concrete grain distributor. After crossing a shallower watercourse, we ignore a track to the left and continue across a grassy glade to a T-junction (Wp.2 20M).

Bearing left at the T-junction, we soon come to a rough turning circle. Our onward route follows the overgrown track to the left, but first we bear right onto a grassy trail marked by a large cairn, and climb to a distinct dent in a large outcrop of limestone, where we find the **Cova de Navarro** (Wp.3 25M), the cave where locals hid when pirates were coming to town, nowadays a refuge for two discarded wheely-bins and dozens of paint tins used as nesting boxes by pigeons. We return by the same path to the turning circle. Take ten minutes off the total time if you skip this side trip.

S'Illot

To continue to the Talaia

We bear left at the turning circle onto the overgrown track, which is so densely immersed in cistus, it looks like a path at first. This track soon ends in its own version of a turning circle, where we bear right (SSE) between the pines.

The way is extremely badly overgrown, so badly overgrown you may suspect there's no way at all, but squeezing between the overgrowth (SSE) alongside a largely invisible watercourse, we emerge (less than 10M from the second turning circle) at the bottom of an open area stripped of vegetation beside some tall, sickly looking pine.

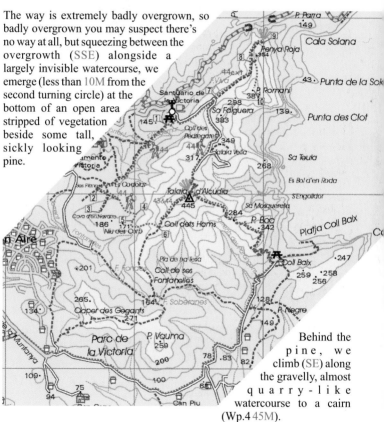

Behind the pine, we climb (SE) along the gravelly, almost quarry-like watercourse to a cairn (Wp.4 45M).

Five metres after the cairn, we bear right, away from the watercourse, to scramble steeply up a very rough animal track for another 20 metres. To our right (SW), we see the shallow depression of a *coll*, and a small cairn perched on a rock midway between us and the *coll*. Fortunately, the vegetation isn't so dense here, as we have a pathless traverse of the hillside to this cairn (Wp.5 55M), after which we maintain direction (SW) to emerge a couple of minutes later a little way above the *coll*, within sight of the large hilltop villa passed on Walk 42.

The *coll* and **Cova Navarro**, which is not far below it, are at the end of a spur branching NW from the main ridge up to the **Talaia**, the western approach used in Walk 43. We bear left now to climb this spur (E). There's still no path, but a number of animal trails wind uphill through increasingly scant vegetation. Towards the top of the spur, we bear right to circle the head of the valley between the spur and the ridge, finally scrambling onto the ridge itself at the base of the main 'spine' described in Walk 43 (Wp.6 80M). We now bear left for a comparatively easy if steep climb to the top, where we can either scramble straight over the rocks at the western end of the summit or bear left to skirt the summit and join the main path from the east (110M)

From the summit, we take the main path (E) to the 'Coll Baix' signpost, where we bear left on a clear, rocky path dropping through impressive switchbacks to the end of the dirt track from the *ermita*. We now follow the dirt track (a dull climb but a pleasantly easy descent after our exertions in the bush) ignoring a branch to the right a couple of minutes later. A gentle descent brings us round the back of the eroded **Sa Falguera** pinnacle down to a distinct U-bend, 30 metres before which is the path on the right to **Penya Roja** and **Puig Romani**, signposted 'Penya des Migdia' (Wp.7 140M).

Extension
The well-trodden **Penya des Migdia** path climbs steadily round the northern side of the peninsula, levelling out briefly before descending (rather more than one would wish after the full circuit) then climbing alongside the crags below **Puig Romani**. A steady climb brings us to a small platform and a junction of paths (Wp.8 15M [from Wp.7).

For Penya Roja
We take the path to the left, which runs alongside the cliffs to the fortifications overlooking **Cap des Pinar**. Squeezing through a tunnel-like entrance to the gun emplacements, where a chain in the rock helps us negotiate a slightly vertiginous section (N.B. Very vertiginous on the way back: if you suffer from vertigo, don't look!), we descend to a natural platform in the middle of the defensive works (Wp.9 5M from Wp.8) to enjoy superb views of **Cap des Pinar**.

For Puig Romani
We bear right at Wp.8 for a short, steep climb up to the **Penya des Migdia** *coll*. Ignoring the clearer, level path, we turn sharp right to climb behind a cairn and scramble up to the asphodel covered summit (Wp.10 15M from Wp.8) for glorious views, including the canon perched rather improbably above the **Penya Roja**. In each case, we return by the same path. The *ermita* is ten minutes from Wp.7 on the main dirt track.

See the notes on GPS use and waypoints on pages 19-20.

28.
The Siller Pass & Serra de la Punta

Wp	N	E
1	39 54.3138	3 04.6446
2	39 54.5634	3 03.9756
3	39 54.7710	3 03.6666
4	39 55.0410	3 03.4488
5	39 55.0926	3 03.7596
6	39 54.8094	3 03.5736
7	39 54.5706	3 03.3042
8	39 54.5112	3 03.2472
9	39 54.3432	3 03.3636
10	39 54.2616	3 03.4374

29.
Lluc - Binifaldó - Lluc

Wp	N	E
1	39 49.2432	2 53.0832
2	39 49.4394	2 53.3820
3	39 50.0202	2 53.7234
4	39 50.1810	2 53.8182
5	39 50.5290	2 54.5898
6	39 50.0400	2 54.7272
7	39 49.6230	2 54.5082
8	39 49.4040	2 54.2544
9	39 49.7544	2 53.8470

30.
Caimari - Lluc - Caimari

Wp	N	E
1	39 46.3632	2 53.9244
2	39 46.5846	2 53.8554
3	39 46.8438	2 53.7996
4	39 47.0820	2 53.7528
5	DELETED	
6	39 47.3616	2 53.6412
7	39 47.8212	2 53.7870
8	39 47.8830	2 53.7744
9	39 47.9526	2 53.4822
10	39 48.3390	2 53.7990
11	39 48.5664	2 53.6088
12	39 48.6630	2 53.4000
13	39 48.9852	2 53.7654
14	39 49.2882	2 54.2340
15	39 49.4034	2 54.2532
16	39 49.6392	2 54.8940
17	39 49.2372	2 55.2102
18	39 49.1190	2 55.5192
19	39 49.0518	2 55.4892
20	39 48.9300	2 55.4364
21	39 48.6030	2 55.0890
22	39 48.2958	2 55.1412
23	39 48.0804	2 55.2924
24	39 47.5662	2 55.1568

31.
Puig Tomir

Wp	N	E
1	39 50.0352	2 54.7380
2	39 50.1180	2 54.9594
3	39 50.2440	2 55.0572
4	39 50.2770	2 55.1352
5	39 50.4480	2 55.3896
6	39 50.5920	2 55.5408
7	39 50.5578	2 55.7028
8	39 50.6292	2 56.0160
9	39 50.5566	2 56.3238
10	39 50.1030	2 56.4414
11	39 49.9500	2 56.1684
12	39 49.7016	2 55.8366
13	39 49.3086	2 55.5444
14	39 49.2132	2 55.2378
15	39 49.1184	2 54.9618
16	39 49.1250	2 54.8700
17	39 49.3476	2 54.2598
18	39 49.6158	2 54.5082

32.
Binifaldó - Pollença

Wp	N	E
1	39 50.3390	2 54.5471
2	39 51.0258	2 55.2234
3	39 51.0978	2 55.5048
4	39 51.0798	2 55.9428
5	39 51.2724	2 56.5488
6	39 52.4922	2 59.5998
7	39 52.9410	3 00.8442

33.
Puig de María

Wp	N	E
1	39 52.3428	3 01.0200
2	39 52.0470	3 01.1844
3	39 52.1478	3 01.3530

34.
L'Havanor

Wp	N	E
1	39 52.0962	2 55.4784
2	39 52.3668	2 55.1964
3	39 52.6062	2 54.7740
4	39 52.4784	2 54.5592
5	39 52.8462	2 54.4272
6	39 53.2296	2 54.0150
7	39 53.1474	2 53.6490
8	39 53.3700	2 54.1812

35.
Rafal d'Ariant & Mortitx Gorge

Wp	N	E
1	39 52.0848	2 55.4718
2	39 52.3692	2 55.4364
3	39 52.5294	2 55.4490
4	39 52.6242	2 55.4688
5	39 52.7562	2 55.4364
6	39 53.0022	2 55.4364
7	39 53.1768	2 55.4196
8	39 53.2296	2 55.4454
9	39 53.5848	2 55.2528
10	39 53.9352	2 55.4004
11	39 53.4546	2 54.9804
12	39 53.2656	2 55.0926
13	39 53.1540	2 55.1712
14	39 52.7917	2 55.2145
15	39 52.5378	2 55.0404

36.
Bóquer Valley

Wp	N	E
1	39 54.6543	3 05.1345
2	39 55.2828	3 05.2242
3	39 55.4610	3 05.4024

37.
Creek & Peak 1 - Na Blanca from Formentor

Wp	N	E
1	39 55.7100	3 08.0880
2	39 55.4874	3 09.2022
3	39 55.9314	3 08.9340

38.
Creek & Peak 2 - El Morro de Catalunya from Cala Figuera

Wp	N	E
1	39 56.8608	3 09.6810
2	39 57.1170	3 10.3812
3	39 57.4374	3 10.3782
4	39 57.4728	3 10.4322
5	39 57.6120	3 10.5666

39.
Creek & Peak 3 - Unnamed summit & Na Blanca from Cala Murta

Wp	N	E
1	39 56.9328	3 10.1784
2	39 56.2752	3 10.9794
3	39 56.4984	3 10.4466
4	39 56.4402	3 09.6576

Wp	N	E	Wp	N	E	Wp	N	E
5	39 56.1060	3 09.2196	3	39 49.8522	3 05.8926	4	39 51.9624	3 10.4142
6	39 55.8486	3 09.2370	4	39 49.9650	3 05.5368	5	39 51.5904	3 11.0892
7	39 55.8642	3 09.4140	5	39 49.6464	3 05.6556	6	39 51.6732	3 11.4258
			6	39 49.4406	3 06.1002	7	39 51.7134	3 11.3046
			7	39 49.6002	3 06.2940			

40.

Creek & Peak 4 - El Fumat, Torrent de les Agulles, & Cala en Gossalba

42.

Alcúdia Peninsula 1 - Ses Fontanelles

44.

Alcúdia Peninsula 3 - Talaia d'Alcúdia & Penya Roja

Wp	N	E	Wp	N	E	Wp	N	E
1	39 57.2478	3 11.3778				1	39 52.3866	3 10.2456
2	39 57.0936	3 11.0700	1	39 51.0684	3 09.3942	2	39 52.0146	3 09.7116
3	39 56.9358	3 10.7736	2	39 51.6936	3 09.5868	3	39 51.8838	3 09.7140
4	39 56.9082	3 10.5426	3	39 51.4014	3 10.1628	4	39 51.8658	3 09.9972
5	39 56.8884	3 10.7490				5	39 51.8394	3 09.9840
6	39 56.5968	3 11.2746				6	39 51.7998	3 10.1964

43.

Alcúdia Peninsula 2 - Coll Baix & Talaia d'Alcúdia

41.

Puig Sant Martí

Wp	N	E	Wp	N	E	Wp	N	E
			1	39 51.4818	3 10.9518	7	39 52.5000	3 10.6134
1	39 49.8774	3 06.2766	2	39 51.2688	3 10.8402	8	39 52.7424	3 10.9080
2	39 49.7358	3 05.9664	3	39 51.4002	3 10.1502	9	39 52.8630	3 11.0052
						10	39 52.6212	3 10.9296

GLOSSARY

This glossary contains Spanish and Catalán words found in the text (shown in *italics*) plus other local words that you may encounter. Please note that the spelling of place names and other local words on signs and maps can vary according to local conventions.

SPANISH	**CATALÁN**	
a		
agua, con/sin gas		water, fizzy/still
aljibe	**aljub**	ancient cistern/reservoir
alto	**dalt**	high, upper
área recreativa		picnic spot, usually with barbecues, toilets, water
atalaya		ancient watch-tower
avenida	**avinguda**	avenue
ayuntamiento	**ayuntament**	town hall
b		
bajo	**baix**	low
bajo	**avall**	lower
barranco	**barranc**	gorge, ravine
botadores		stone steps in country walls
c		
cala		creek, small bay, sometimes just a tiny coastal indentation
cala		inlet, cove
calle	**carrer**	street
camino	**camí**	road, path or way
camino real	**camí real**	royal road, once a major donkey trail
campo		countryside, field
canaleta	**siquia**	man-made water channel, including anything from a concrete canal to delicately arched aqueducts
carritx		pampas-like grass
casa	**can/ca**	house of (as *chez* in French)
casa de nieve	**casa neu**	snow pit/ice house
caseta		hut, cabin, small house

cingles		cliffs, crags; most often used to describe the sort of short, abrupt cliffs that typically define the rounded summits of many Catalán and Mallorcan mountains
ciudad	**ciutat**	city
coll		saddle, neck or pass
correos		post office
costa		coast

e

embalse		reservoir
ermita		hermitage, small church, shrine

f

faro		lighthouse
fiesta		festival, public holiday
finca	**lluc**	farm
forn de calç	**horno de calç**	lime kiln
fuente	**font**	spring, well

l

lavadero		public laundry area
llano	**pla**	plain, flat land

m

medio	**mig**	middle
mercado	**mercat**	market
mirador		viewing point, sometimes with man-made facilities, more often a natural place with a good view
morro		snout or muzzle, a rounded summit

p

parada		bus stop
particular		private
paseo	**passeig**	walkway
peatones		pedestrians
peña	**penya/penyal**	rock or boulder, used for a knoll or pinnacle on a ridge
pico	**puig**	translates as 'hill' or 'height', though more often a peak or mountain
pista		dirt road
pista forestal		forest road
playa	**platja**	beach
plaza	**plaça**	town square
pozo	**pou**	well
privado		private
prohibido el paso		no entry
puerto	**port**	port, mountain pass

r

refugio		mountain refuge, some offering basic overnight accommodation

s

santo/a	**san/sant**	saint
santuario	**santuari**	monastery, hermitage
sendero	**senda**	footpath, trail
sitja (pl. sitjes)	**sitja**	charcoal burning area or circle
su	**son, sa, ses**	his, her, their

t

tipico		typical, locals' café/bar
toro bravo		wild bull
torre		tower, often a coastal watchtower built to warn of approaching pirates, or a Moorish lookout tower
torrente	**torrent**	stream

u

urbanización		housing development

BIBLIOGRAPHY

General books in English
  Wild Olives William Graves (Hutchinson) What Dad did after all that.
  Snowball Oranges Peter Kerr (Summersdale) Peter Mayle, Chris
      Stewart &c. &c.
  A Winter In Majorca George Sand (various editions) Bitter about
      Mallorcans.
Locally published books in English
  Folk Tales of Mallorca Mn. Alcover (Moll)
  Wild Orchids of Mallorca Nicole T. Beniston & William S. Beniston
      (Moll)
  Plants of the Balearic Islands Anthony Boner (Moll)
  Bread & Oil* and **A Home in Majorca**** Tomás Graves
      *(Prospect) **(Foradada)
  Birds of the Balearic Islands Joan Mayol (Moll)
  Discovering the Art of Mallorcan Cooking Toby Molenar (Moll)
  Majorca, The Island of Calm Santiago Rusiñol
Walking Guides in English
  Walking in Mallorca June Parker (Cicerone)
All ramblers in Mallorca owe a huge debt to June Parker, who first
described many routes even the locals hadn't published.
  Holiday Walks in Mallorca Graham Beech (Sigma)
  Landscapes of Mallorca Valerie Crespí-Green (Sunflower)
  Mallorca Rolf Goetz (Rother)
Walking Guides in Catalán
Lluis Vallcanares has published several guides, including three volumes of
itineraries suitable for children ***Descobrim Tramuntana*** (Gorg Blau) (Vol. 1.
6-8 years old, Vol. 2. 8-10 years old, Vol. 3. 10-12 years old) and two volumes
of 20 ***Itineraris Alternatius*** (Gorg Blau) featuring several routes like the Es
Racó ascent of the Teix massif that I felt weren't appropriate for a walking
guide.

APPENDIX A

CYCLING ROUTES
Off-Road
Compared to mainland Spain, Mallorca is not a great place for off-road
cycling, though the following dirt tracks are suitable:
① Mirador de ses Barques to Coll de Biniamar (see Walk 14)
② Bunyola - Cas Garriguer - Es Cocons - Bunyola (see Walk 25)
③ Alaró to Pla Espot (see Walk 26)
④ Lloseta to Tossals Verds (see Walk 17)
⑤ Fonts d'es Noguera to the pumping station following the new *canaleta*
(see   Walk 18)
⑥ Caimari to Lluc (see Walk 31)
⑦ Massanella/Son Catlar to Comafreda/Lluc via Coll de Sa Linia (see
      Appendix D)
⑧ Port de Pollença to Cala St. Vicenç via Coll de Siller (Walk 29)
⑨ Alcúdia to Coll Baix via Camí de la Muntanya (see Walk 43)
⑩ Alcúdia to the base of the Talaia de Alcúdia (see Walk 45 short version
(b))

Tarmac

Road cycling, however, is another matter. There are so many bikes that some roads have signposts specifically for cyclists. Among the most popular routes are:

①	C-710	Sóller – Lluc – Pollença
②	C-711	Sóller – Bunyola
③	PM-210	Bunyola –Orient – Alaró
④	PM-211	Alaró – Lloseta
⑤	PM-211-3&4	Lloseta – Selva
⑥	PM-213	Selva – Lluc
⑦	PM-220-1	Pollença-Alcúdia
⑧	PM-221	Port de Pollença – Cap de Formentor

Bikes can be rented in Port de Sóller, Port de Pollença and Playa de Alcúdia

APPENDIX B

USEFUL INFORMATION

The code for Spain is 34. When dialling from the U.K. prefix this with 00.
Phone numbers below are shown in red, email/web addresses in green.

ACCOMMODATION

Getting A Bed

The following suggestions are just a selection from the wide range of choices available.

www.mallorca.com/english

Shallow Pockets

Ermitas & *refugio*s: a full list is available from Tourist Information offices, but the following are on itineraries in the book:

Walks 43-5	**Ermita de la Victòria**	971 549912
Walks 31-3	**Santuario de Lluc**	971 871525
Walk 34	**Santuario del Puig de Maria**	971 184132
Walk 26	**Castell de Alaró**	971 182112
Walk 9	**Refugio La Muleta**	971 634271

www.conselldemallorca.net/muleta

Walks 17&18   **Refugio Tossals Verds** 971 182027

www.conselldemallorca.net/tossals

Middling Pockets

Hotel Brisas	971 631352
Hotel/Apartments Generoso	971 631450
Hotel Sóller Garden	971 638046
Hotel Miramar	971 631350

Deep Pockets

L'Hermitage, Orient www.hermitage-hotel.com info@hermitage-hotel.com

Es Molí, Deià   www.hotelesmoli.com   www.esmoli.com
reservas@esmoli.com

S'Olivaret, Alaró   www.solivaret.com   info@solivaret.com

GETTING ABOUT

Ask in Tourist Offices for current timetables. Winter services are much less frequent than in the main season of around April to the end of October. For general travel information see:

www.mallorca.com/english

Boats   **Buses**
www.barcosazules.com
www.autocaresmallorca.com
Ferries   **Trains**
www.trasmediterranea.es   www.trensdesoller.com

USEFUL ADDRESSES & TELEPHONE NUMBERS
Miscellaneous
Emergencies   Tel. 112

General Information on the Internet
www.ensaimadablau.com   www.balearnet.com
www.visitbalears.com
www.mallorca.com/english
www.mallorcaservice.com   www.caib.es
Consell de Mallorca   www.conselldemallorca.net
Meteorology www.inm.es/cmt/palm **Tourist Guides**
www.apitmallorca.com

APPENDIX C

RECOMMENDED ADDRESSES
A full guide to services is not part of our brief, but...
If you're arriving late, leaving early, or are otherwise delayed at the airport, there's an adequate hotel (**Portofino** 971 260464 jovemarsl@yahoo.es) and a good restaurant (**Granja Marina**) on Calle Trafalgar in the Ciudad Jardin at **Coll d'en Rebassa**, next to the airport.

Hotel Brisas, **Port de Sóller** – a good basic hotel with facilities and food to the same standard €45 B&B for two, 971 631352 **Sóller Jardin**, **Port de Sóller** – excellent value €23 pp B&B, €28 half-board. Family friendly, butlinesque chalets, and an evening buffet, outstanding for €5. www.sollergarden.com 971 638046

If you're staying in a cheap hotel near **Sóller** and are suffering from LYLF (Liptons Yellow Label Fatigue) a decent cup of tea can be had at the **Luna 36** bar, **Carrer sa Lluna**, while the **Bar Turismo** on **Carrer Born** pulls off the difficult trick of being at once sophisticated, friendly and authentically local.

Cafeteria Don Juan on **Port de Sóller** seafront is a basic picture-menu tourist restaurant also used by locals. The **Pizzeria de Porto** on **Port de Sóller** seafront serves good quality 'real' pizzas. Excellent Mallorcan cuisine is available at **Ca's Missèr** in **Selva**.

Highly recommended is the excellent **Bon Cami Trekking, Outdoor and Adventure Shop**. You'll find it on Calle Roger de Flor No.36, **Port de Pollença** 07470. In addition to a stocking a wide range of books, clothing and equipment, Suzanne and Jaume are experts on Mallorca and may be able to advise on accessibility of routes.

WHAT GOT LEFT OUT (OR ALMOST LEFT OUT) AND WHY

The following classic routes have been closed: the **Son Coll** path to **Deià**, the **Alfábia Ridge** from **S'Arrom**, **L'Ofre** from **Orient** (theoretically still possible but practically too great a gauntlet), the **Alcaldena**, the **Ternelles Valley**, and the **Cuixat Gorge**.

Walks 19 and 28

Please note that, while still passable, some access difficulties have been reported by users of this book's first edition on these routes.

The path from **Mancor del Valle** to **Tossals Verds** via **Es Rafals** is still theoretically open and is officially signposted from the top, but you may not receive a friendly reception from the landowner.

La Muleta and **Teix** from **Coll de Sóller** are included though parts of them are under threat (see individual itineraries for details).

The following routes have been excluded because access is limited to Sundays or seasonally restricted: **Puig Roig**, **Puig Caragoler de Femenia**, **Torre de Lluc** via **Coscona**, **Torrent de Lluc** via **Clot d'Albarca**, and **La Mola** from **Cala St. Vicenç**.

The **L'Havanor** and **Mortitx Gorge** routes are included, though access is restricted in April/May during the Black Vulture breeding season.

The **Cuculla de Fartatrix** and **Puig de Ca** itineraries are not described as they involve crossing fields full of *toros bravos*.

Lost paths blight the attractive looking circuit round **Puig Balitx** appearing on some maps. The descent to **Coll d'en Marques** via **Can Boscos** is blocked by a spiked gate at the 398 metre coll.

The **Mitx Dia** below **Puig Major**, which is in any case a little challenging for a book like this, has been excluded as there is a potential for conflict, not with the military who used to vet access, but depending on who has leased the hunting rights in any given season. The **Can Boqueta** and **Es Racó** ascents of the Teix massif were also deemed inappropriate for a book of this nature.

The **Racó d'en Barona** ascent of **Puig Moro** and the two charcoal burners' routes climbing from the C-711 above the tunnel (at km27 and **Fuente de la Reina**) may be possible for determined individuals, but have been excluded from the book due to obvious efforts to block access.

As a matter of principle, classic itineraries that now involve payment for access have been excluded. Nonetheless, principles tend to be compromised, and it must be said that the huge **Massanella Adventure Centre**, which extends from **Comafreda** in the north (the traditional route between **Lluc**, **Puig Massanella** and **Gorg Blau**) to **Mancor** in the south, and which charges €4 for access, seems to be using the money to some purpose, improving facilities and maintaining paths. Walk 27 details a way into this area without paying, but I wouldn't want to be accused of discouraging an initiative that's considerably more positive than buying a padlock and a *prohibido el paso* sign, and which may well be a model for the future of walking in Mallorca, so here is a brief description of one paying way into the estate (N.B. Numerous alternative cairn-marked paths branch off this route between 0M & 55M offering ample opportunity for further exploration):

THE CANALETA FROM MANCOR DES VALLES

Timing: 3-4 hours   Distance: discretionary
Altitude Climbed: 500 metres   Exertion: 5
Refreshment: 3 at **Can Bajoca** (closed Mondays)

Parking (and paying!) at the **Son Catlar** restaurant on the **Mancor-Caimari** road (0M), take the broad dirt track passing the **Can Bajoca Refuge** bar/restaurant (25M). Continue along the track into the impressive gorge, going through a gateway and passing a stone cabin beside a long stone corral. At a well-maintained *casa forestal* fronted by a canopied picnic area (55M), leave the track (which continues to **Coll de sa Linia** joining the traditional **Massanella-Lluc** trail and Walk 28), and bear left into a fine oak forest on a broad walking trail that soon dwindles to a path marked with cairns and red waymarks (65M).

The path climbs (forever!) passing a Y-junction (75M) (the two routes rejoin but the left branch is easier) and crossing a stile, before reaching the celebrated *canaleta* (95M) –cobbled together, so the story goes, by a local pig farmer when the specialists were stumped by the engineering problems. Bear right and follow the *canaleta* as far as your own personal arrangement with vertigo allows. Mine let me get about halfway, but if you have a good head for heights you can continue all the way to **Tossals Verds** and even **Gorg Blau** or **Cúber**. The descent from 95M by the same route takes a little over an hour.

The **Tossals Verds** Circuit is included although there is a possibility of being asked to pay to cross private land.

Map sections used in this book are adapted from Mallorca North & Mountains Tour & Trail Super-Durable Map.
ISBN 1-899554-93-9
(£7.99)

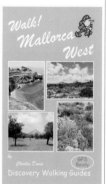

If you've enjoyed this book, we recommend its companion volume Walk! Mallorca West.
ISBN 1-899554-98-X
(£11.99)

For a full list of our titles see our websites:
www.walking.demon.co.uk and **www.dwgwalking.co.uk**
- or for a catalogue and current newsletter send a C5 size envelope with a 47p stamp, addressed to yourself to:
Discovery Walking Guides Ltd.
10 Tennyson Close
Northampton NN5 7HJ

Please note that the spelling of place names and other local words on signs and maps can vary according to local conventions; Castilian and Mallorquin versions are frequently different..